T0247808

## *Praise for* SIGHTLINES FROM THE CHEAP SEATS

"Musical, muscular, romantic, wise, Joseph Di Prisco's new collection of poems, *Sightlines from the Cheap Seats* offers an expansive view of the landscape, taking us on a curvy trail out of the stadium that leads to our hearts and minds—a poetry adventure that kicks down doors to hidden rooms filled with sunlight."

—Kim Dower, *Last Train to the Missing Planet*

"*Sightlines From the Cheap Seats* is a big book full of sharp, funny takes on directions, lists, résumés, mission statements—the documents that spread across our lives. The exuberance of Di Prisco's voice is exhilarating. He'll spin out an image or a catalogue about as far as it will go, then take it farther still. Puns abound. Joseph Di Prisco is the commander of the comic turn, the pasha of absurd hyperbole. No need for an appointment—the satrap will see you now."

—Don Bogen, *An Algebra*

## *Praise for* POEMS IN WHICH

"Somehow the speaker in Joseph Di Prisco's new poems manages to install himself in the kitchenware of contemporary culture without becoming a part of it. With a wit that questions as it embraces, *Poems in Which* provides us with a strong, original voice."

—Carl Dennis, winner of the Pulitzer Prize

"This is a joyous book. Even addressing unquenchable longing and the shadows of death and failure, the lyric engines of these poems propel us with vital combustions. Operatic, in that suffering and sadness are sung with the same gusto and octave-expanse as triumph and discovery, this work is proof of the presence of a large, funny and indefatigable spirit."

—Dean Young

"Di Prisco mixes the immiscible: an authentic lyric voice and a sense of the self (and world) as dispersed and constructed. His poems are funny, smart, and moving; they quiz the options they exercise but are never coy."

—Guy Rotella

errors, confronting friends and enemies. This is a novel about posthumous discoveries, reunions and revenge. Readers of J. F. Powers's *Morte d'Urban* and Alice McDermott's *Charming Billy* should find their way to *All For Now*."

—P. F. Kluge, author of *A Call From Jersey*, *Gone Tomorrow*, and *Eddie and the Cruisers*

"Joseph Di Prisco has given us a brave, bumbling, soul-searching hero whose wry humor only enhances his honesty."

—Jan Weissmiller, Owner, Prairie Lights Books

## *Praise for* POPE OF BROOKLYN

"A literary son traces his fugitive father in a pulpy yet cerebral memoir... This sprawling narrative is punctuated by Di Prisco's reflections on literature, faith, mortality, and his own tangled romances and outré experiences, ranging from cocaine addiction to mentoring adolescents.... Deft, amusing, and tough."

—*Kirkus Reviews*

## *Praise for* THE GOOD FAMILY FITZGERALD

"Di Prisco has gone out on a limb with his family history, reminiscent in many ways of Irwin Shaw's Rich Man, Poor Man, casting this big fat gem of a book out on a vast ocean of literary 'minimalism'. At a time when 'restraint' is one of the buzzwords in contemporary fiction, he's given us a tome almost as big as the New Testament. But it's definitely more profane than sacred. And it's mesmerizing."

—Anne Cunningham

"Joseph di Prisco's new novel, *The Good Family Fitzgerald*, is a sprawling saga of an Irish-American clan, a richly comedic drama with indelible characters, told with biting wit.... His Fitzgeralds are by turns hot-headed and enigmatic, bursting with vitality or keeping their thoughts to themselves. The plot is episodic but compelling, and the dialogue clever without becoming cutesy. *The Good Family Fitzgerald* is a book worth sinking into, well-suited for relaxing in a hammock on a lazy afternoon."

—Michael Berry, Berkeleyside

"A Fantastic Russian Novel Ingeniously Cast with Irish Americans: You will enjoy a rich experience with this book just taking in the page-after-page feast of Di Prisco's social and behavioral observations—every bit as trenchant and funny as those of

Tom Wolfe at his best.... *The Good Family Fitzgerald* is no less than a vast Russian novel (with, incidentally, a fraction of the heart-clogging misery and suffering calories) that, perhaps taking a page from Hamilton, is refreshingly, ingeniously cast with Irish Americans. Highly recommended!"

—Lawrence G. Townsend, author of *The Hot Monkey Love Trial*

## Praise for SIBELLA & SIBELLA

"Joseph Di Prisco's fearlessness always impresses me, and his latest novel is no exception. Invoking satire and silliness, bad puns and good ones, hijinks and hilarity, *Sibella & Sibella* takes on the absurdity of publishing, narrated through the lens of a young woman working as a junior editor at a San Francisco publishing house. Fortunately for readers, Di Prisco embraces the absurdity, and the result is this wonderfully crafted and bitingly funny critique that never fails to entertain."

—Lori Ostlund, award-winning author of *After the Parade*

"In the rarified realm of A Confederacy of Dunces and David Markson's *Wittgenstein's Mistress*, *Sibella & Sibella* is surely the new picaresque—set in the mysterious world of independent publishing, the singular voice of a junior editor is roundly inhabited by Mr. Di Prisco who nimbly plays with form and language, and an industry he clearly both loves and scorns. A remarkable reading experience."

—David Francis, author of *Stray Dog Winter* and *Wedding Bush Road*

## Praise for THE ALZHAMMER

"Part Mafia thriller, part comic farce, part lament about the anguish of dementia and all hyperkinetic.... Fast-paced and often charming."

—*Kirkus Reviews*

"Di Prisco writes with humor and a great sense of character, poking fun at things that would leave a lesser author cringing. Think *Cuckoo's Nest* meets *The Godfather*. He interweaves all these elements with the skill of a master writer."

—Anne Hillerman, *New York Times* bestselling author of
*Spider Woman's Daughter* and *Rock with Wings*

"Great funny lines on every page. Am I recommending *The Alzhammer*? As the protagonist Mikey might say, 'Eggs ackly.'"

—Jack Handey, author of *Deep Thoughts*

# MY LAST RESUME

# ALSO BY JOSEPH DI PRISCO

## Poetry

*Wit's End*
*Poems in Which*
*Sightlines from the Cheap Seats*

## Memoir

*Subway to California*
*The Pope of Brooklyn*

## Fiction

*Confessions of Brother Eli*
*Sun City*
*All for Now*
*The Alzhammer*
*(Or: Keep Your Friends Close and I Forget the Other Thing)*
*Sibella & Sibella*
*The Good Family Fitzgerald*

## Nonfiction

*Field Guide to the American Teenager (with Michael Riera)*
*Right from Wrong (with Michael Riera)*

# EDITED BY JOSEPH DI PRISCO

*Simpsonistas: Tales from the Simpson Literary Project (Vol. 1)*
*Simpsonistas: Tales from the Simpson Literary Project (Vol. 2)*
*Simpsonistas: Tales from the Simpson Literary Project (Vol. 3)*
*Simpsonistas: Tales from New Literary Project (Vol. 4)*
*Simpsonistas: Tales from New Literary Project (Vol. 5)*

# JOSEPH DI PRISCO
# MY LAST RESUME
## NEW & COLLECTED POEMS
### *1971–1980 | 1999–2023*

RARE BIRD
LOS ANGELES, CALIF.

RARE BIRD

THIS IS A GENUINE RARE BIRD BOOK

Rare Bird Books
6044 North Figueroa Street
Los Angeles, CA 90042
rarebirdbooks.com

For more information, address:
Rare Bird Books Subsidiary Rights Department
6044 North Figueroa Street
Los Angeles, CA 90042

Set in Minion
Printed in the United States

Wit's End *originally published by University of Missouri Press (1975)*
Poems In Which *originally published by Bear Star Press (2000)*
Sightlines From the Cheap Seats *originally published by Rare Bird Books (2017)*

10 9 8 7 6 5 4 3 2 1

Library of Congress Cataloging-in-Publication Data available upon request

# CONTENTS

# WIT'S END (1975)  197

## THE STARLIKE EXPRESS: NEW POEMS   261

*For Patti*

# SIGHTLINES FROM THE CHEAP SEATS

*To Aidan, Damon, & Kenna*

**PART ONE**

# MY LAST RESUME

When I was a troubadour
When I was an astronaut
When I was a pirate
You should have seen my closet
You would have loved my shoes.
Kindly consider my application
Even though your position is filled.
This is my stash of snow globes
This is my favorite whip
This is a picture of me with a macaw
This is a song I almost could sing.
When I was a freight train
When I was a satellite
When I was a campfire
You should have seen the starburst
You should have tasted my tomato.
I feel sorry for you I'm unqualified
This is my finest tube of toothpaste
This is when I rode like the raj on a yak
This is the gasoline this is the match.
When I was Hegel's dialectic
When I was something Rothko forgot
When I was moonlight paving the street
You should have seen the roiling shore
You should have heard the swarm of bees.

# MORE ELEMENTS OF STYLE

*"I forgive everyone and ask forgiveness of everyone. OK? Don't gossip
too much."*
*"Perdono tutti e a tutti chiedono perdono. Va bene? Non fate troppi
pettegolezzi."*
*Cesare Pavese's suicide note, 26 August 1950*

"Hopefully" is an adverb meaning "full of hope."
You may write "You hopefully received the thousand red roses"
If you're dating the New Year's Day Parade in Pasadena.
Omit needless words except for *susurration* and *gash*
*Gold-vermilion*. Hold nothing back. Spend every cent.
Next morning, look hard at what you have left behind.
You'll be surprised—if you're like me, and you're not—
At the missed opportunities and water marks on the page.
Avoid inert gasses and verbs. Having is overrated,
And being only goes so far, not that I need tell you now.
There's no such thing as rewriting, you know,
Only writing. That's about as helpless as I can be.
Don't be discouraged when the piano tuner stops to eat
His hero sandwich over the keys. It's all part of the process,
A messy fugue. You are in this way one with
Everyone who ever penned a word. Sometimes,
Words like loved ones fail you, it's not their fault.
Sometimes you fail them, and it is.
Before long you may hear the piano chords played
In a far-off room, and you may feel a sadness

That lights within, a candle inside a carved pumpkin
All Hallow's Eve. This is normal. You're not, and no one is.
Sometimes the best writers break all the rules,
They make comma splices sing, they don't know they are
The best writers, and they just can't wait around to find out.
May I commend you on your use of concrete language
And your personal voice, petals on a wet black bough.
Read your work out loud, to others, or to yourself,
For you must listen to the music, the echo, the ping
Of conviction like a sonar signal under the sea.
Some nights are a sea and we are all submerged.
The moon makes tides, the man you are walks
A new shore and leaves footprints that are never erased.
Do not overstate, do not explain, be emphatic at the close.
This world is not for everyone, that much is unclear.
The other world calls out, saying come home,
You will be welcomed, there's nothing more
Hopefully left to be said, gash gold-vermilion.
Make sure your reader knows who is speaking to whom.

# THE RINGLING BROS BARNUM
## AND MY FAMILY CIRCUS

Bengal tigers don't naturally leap through rings of fire,
They must be trained, they must be abused,
Unlike my brother, who held the hoop and leaped
At the same time as if he had been born to do that
And he was. I myself am the Bearded Lady
Because there were no volunteers,
Which was all right, given the epaulets
That graced my dress blues. Animal rights activists
Make a good point. Don't tase Dumbo,
You slimy circus bastards, or my brother,
Who would not shoot you with a real gun.
My mom walked the tightrope with balance beam,
How else to reach the other side?
My dad was impatient below, arms folded, in case.
People fear the clown, but clowns are terrified of them.
Their cars run in circles, on pharmaceutical fumes.
Saturday my family circus showed for the funeral,
A regular stop on the tour. Smell of popcorn
Filled the air, like Iowa, cotton candy bloomed
In everyone's tiny hands like cherry blossom,
A tornado touched down, the big top exhaled.

# ADVENTURES IN LANGUAGE SCHOOL

Rome: such a great city for walking unless
You are hit by a car, as I was tonight, though it was only
A tiny car. The cretino driver had my language progress
In mind as I practiced my idioms and gestures,
Like what they call "holding the umbrella"
(don't ask, think about it). The driver's eyes
Told me I had a long way to go if I wished to
Score a point about livestock and his love life.
Still, a sorrowful ghostly city like Rome is good
For dying if it came to that, so many spaces
For monuments, someday maybe one of Me in Language
School, in full command of the imperfect subjunctive,
Which is called the Congiuntivo Imperfetto,
Which sounds like a coffee or pasta but is not.
Later this night a girl in a moonlight-swathed piazza,
Unlit cigarette at her fingertips, asks in her English,
"Have you a fire for me?" Sometimes even Italian fails.
You won't believe how much you use the Congiuntivo
Imperfetto during foreplay, painting a ceiling, or when hit
By a car. Night times I spent in the Piazza dell'
Orologio—*orologio* means clock—sweepingly
Subjunctive and imperfect, and studied the big clock
On the tower, the one with missing hands,
And appreciated anew Italians' conceptions of love
And death and why they were always late.
I am the oldest student in the class by a factor of two.

Also the only male, by a factor of no idea. The Russians
Have atrocious accents but their grammar and miniskirts
Are exceptional, especially with the subjunctive mood.
The goal is to think in Italian, to speak without
Thinking, so I am halfway home. Maybe it was my toga
That turned the teacher against me. I ask her to go
With me to the Coliseum, where everyone soon dies,
As I will, which is why I first came to Rome.
The most beautiful girl in school is from Algiers.
Her black eyes demand I reexamine my whole life.
Oh, the things I could tell you about language school
Would fill a book, a little grammar exercise book
Specializing in the imperfect subjunctive, required
Every second in Rome especially while sitting next
To a gorgeous sweet Algerian girl named Sisi,
Which in Italian sounds like *si, si*, yes, yes.
That's why, if I have to live, Rome is not so bad,
It's such a sad city, with the best art over my head,
Cars so small that afterward I run back to language school.

# REASONS NOBODY EVER CALLED
# A GOOD BOOK OF POEMS
# A PAGE-TURNER

Your first dog is ever your one dog
And no story has a happy ending anymore.
We have all wasted lives, sometimes we waste
Our own. Some nights are long ones, some
Never end at all. I don't know how we can
*fall* in love, which implies landing,
Whereas love promises everything but.
That's why I like to listen to birds call
At dusk to each other from the acacias
But then I recall it's still daylight and I
Hear them in the absence of the trees.
When I am traveling by train over mountains
All I think of is the sea. My father was
Never quite so alive until he died and now
He's immortal. Somebody must do the calculus,
Somebody must work out the logic of the logic
Of this spectacle because spectacle's the last
Word anyone would use for dreams that don't cease,
For the sound of weeping coming from the next room,
Only there's no next room and we're the only ones
There, though just for a moment and a lifetime more.
Listen, I will tell you a secret, the secret you told
Me once on the train into the mountains
On the journey to the shore, a time long ago when
We spoke and never met. *That* secret, which is ours.

Some nights are so long the old dog comes home
To us who remain there waiting and waiting
Even if we've never been here before, where we are.

## SLEEP IS/IS NOT A LOST CAUSE

I needed new sightlines from the cheap seats.
Travel had to be sweeter than the night
Glued to the lampshade inside my head,
Since the knockout in the first round.

Soon I'm jetting to Rome, fondling strangers
Securely bereft of their expensive clothes.
I'm ordering the tripe, the oxtail, the brains,
Washing it down with caldrons of grappa.

That's why I count on being seriously sick.
The world is a strange place, that's for sure.
I can't subscribe to the existence of space
Aliens, though, I've been hurt before.

Tough to read *The Divine Comedy* on a Vespa
Or write it. If Dante drove a Vespa the history
Of the world literature would be revised.
Can't help I'm singing some aria, drunk.

Let's suffer blackouts together, boygirls and gargoyles.
Now the stars swirl in the whirlpool of
The looking glass. Cannot wait for day to break
Inside my diving bell, cuttlefish cling to the spire.

# LADY, WITH HIPPOPOTAMUS

Seems one night slipped the hippopotamus
Into her home and next day was Christmas, ho ho.
In other news they exhumed Neruda while
A quartet played stately music on the sands of
Isla Negra. Officials wanted to determine for sure
If he'd been poisoned, but tests came in no.
Belief is a Chinese firecracker popcorning in
Your grasp. About that woman: she was smart
And she blew on pinwheels at every chance
And put her shoes in the oven to sleep
And showered twice a week in her pink PJs
If we didn't catch her first and she moved fast.
She had early onset dementia and apparently now
That hippo. We loved her and she loved Christmas
So I told her I wanted a pony this year.
She said she'd see what she could do, but first
There was a jittery hippo in the living room, which
Would get in Santa's way on this mid-summer night.
Let's review. People wire cash to a Nigerian prince
Exiled in London with email so as to claim
A fortune in misplaced diamonds and some fall
In love with serial killers on death row so don't
Give me grief about her one measly hippopotamus
Or Neruda's resurrection or Three Wise Men at the manger.
That was the night she called 911 on the hippo.
After silence long as Saturday lines at the DMV

They dispatched a squad car and two cops.
Long-term memory being the marbly vault it is,
Once upon a time she'd been a professor, so she got
A broom and prodded the hippo into the corner,
The way she dealt with department rivals before.
In a zoo a hippo looks lazy and slow, jolly and
Oafish as a cartoon. Not so in the jungle.
That huge herbivorous mammal runs faster than you
And will bite off your head and shoulders if you come
Between it and a calf, and river bottoms are strewn
With the wreckage of boats that dared interrupt
A morning swim. Nobody at the academy had
Trained the cops to confront a lady like that's
Hippopotamus, and there it was in plain sight—
Only they had another name for her hippopotamus.
They called it a *possum*, which was close enough.
So they moved around chairs and boxes and made
An escape route out the front door. It took a while
But then they shivered as the possum snarled
And hissed, pink tail twitching, when it scurried
Out into the clear Christmas Eve night air.
That done, she asked the nice officers to help
Her find and decorate a tree. There were
Presents to roast and cookies to paint
And carols to string up and lights to sing
And oh yes, a pony to buy at the pony store.
But the cops were sorry, an elephant was loose nearby
And that was OK, she had the rest of her life
To get right what was always now a little bit wrong.
Merry Christmas to all, leaving her they cried out,
And to all in a brain blizzard good night, good night.

# EULOGIST ON CALL

Some kind of world it was it was.
So here is that fallen leaf lake you dream
All next day you dreamt, the dream
That shakes you out like liar's dice.
Yes, we're all unhinged, but some of us
Are doors. We gather by that lake
Where skittish palominos drink, where
Raptor shadows on the hillside fly.
Ripples running on the surface:
Unread pages deckle-edged.
There is nothing left to explain.
The piano drifts on lily pads. Who put
The harvest in the barn is immaterial,
As am I. Long are the orchards,
Hollow is the house with echoing steps.
Here it is always autumn and the coats
Are perfect and you're ravenous not for food.
It's true a terrible mistake's been made
But it's not the one you thought. Nobody born
Ever had a Plan B, this was not your fault.
I see your face sketched upon the lake,
And water has become your last name.

# MY PORNOGRAPHY PROBLEM

Snapping on latex gloves clears the mind,
And lives of mystics are overrated, though not by me.
You need to define problem, need to define porn.
The world is Christmas-treed with pixels
And pop-ups, let's have a look. Desire is visual,
Maybe a new pill will again make me blind.
That time in Pompeii I got lost in the brothel
Where saved frescoes depict the menus for
The doomed, don't I know it, before the great
Eruption, when people swam in lava, choked down
Clouds of dust. Western Civilization, I rest
My case. Is that your handy Catullus or are you
Begging for it? I did not fail Philosophy One
Oh One for nothing, I failed it for everything.
Everybody's talking about zombies once more,
The nutritional benefits of flax seed and kale,
The balance achieved through Tai Qi.
I'm not here to argue about the body, I'm not
Here at all, I'm there, in the clearing, a risky place
That's not a place and the body is a beautiful thing,
Not that it's a thing. I'll tell you what happens to
Time, but not now, now I'm pulling out knives
From my eyes, now I'm tracking down my breath
From the snow summit. Before I was disembodied
The klieg lights unforgave me, afterward
I poked my head up through the recollected rubble.

The body is a factory, an internal combustion engine,
An electrical network and a jeweled temple, a planet
And a satellite with alternate day parking.
Monks and their out-of-body experience—nice work
If you can get it. Shakespeare the Bard thought love
Located in the liver, OK history's cruel, he also called
Ejaculated semen *spirit* so he's being unhelpful
For a change. Mind and body may possibly exist
Along a continuum, Philosophy Menage a Two-ah.
The Amazon River's kind of a continuum
With predatory fish and neonized birds and hostile
Indigenous tribes that thwack your kayak from
The banks, so hold that thought. Along about
Now I can almost hear somebody posit the soul:
This party must be coming fast to a close.
Some bodies are luminous, some gauzy numinous.
If you want to talk dirty, I will completely understand.

# NAPOLI, NAPOLI

Garbage strike in Napoli, bella bella Napoli.
Castel Nuovo, drone of flies, orange-egg-yolk-sun,
Life is perfetta, quasi. Someone's broken into song,
Chances are it's me, threatened be the throng.
Strangers exchange reckless wedding vows,
Small arms fire, black market currency, cheese,
They can't shout down my "Nessun Dorma," it's Napoli.
See, the reason there are garbage strikes is that
Kingpin mobsters have lost their way. Skins
Of bananas and wine bottle shards make them want
To kill each other some more—you know, *mobsters*?
Meanwhile, fortune tellers in turbans set up shop.
He will get the corner office, she will find
The lost cat safe under her bed. They predict success
For me, just not in this lifetime or in Napoli.
I will, despite myself, endure for one moment
Impossible joy. I decree: Garbage strike, over.
Gangsters, seize brush and canvas, your black beret.
Fisherman, drag in the haul of your crustaceous life.
Where'd this red Vespa come from? Like I care.
A shimmering fish with a death wish turns into my soul mate,
Wraps her evolutionarily mixed-up mitts around my eyes,
We zoom through trash into the soup that's the sea.

# THERE COMES A TIME THERE COMES A TIME
## *OR:*
## GO FORTH

Never order eel in a bistro with your girlfriend
In a land once called France thirty-five years
Ago when afterward you make a solemn vow—
Acid, never again. For certain that's the night
Van Gogh Van Gogh'd the sky, thirty-five
Years, a minute, ago. I'd lost touch with her
And the continent since then. You know,
My investment banking career, Constance
And my four rug rats and pugs, keeping up
With the Fractals, the movie moguls next door.
College is a time to take risks, to work hard,
To eat an eel in France with your girlfriend,
Who's fucking half the Sorbonne,
While you scheme on the other half.
College was wonderful, I hear, and I have
One photograph of her for proof.
Never did learn the college fight song
But I could fake it like some orgasms
I don't need to revisualize. About
Her photo, she's still wearing the crimson
Scarf and would you believe her picture
Was still on my desk alongside the model
Train set when she left me a voice
Mail? Yes, time is a funny thing, but I still
Harbor a grudge against Daylight Savings,

Marching through the house to disarm
The bomb in each device. Why so many clocks?
And all set to the same redundant hour,
Which I chalk up to missed opportunity.
So tonight I know where she is (phone,
Voice mail), but not where I am anymore,
Which is oddly how I might prefer
My eel these days. She has not changed one
Iota. Me? Time works on me like water,
Leaving less and less and thankfully less
In its wake. When I listen to her voice
Mail, my ear opens up to let her slither
Phosphorescent inside, a nice look
On her. I think I will save her message
For the rest of my life, which I have already
Squandered, long after eel and starry night
And the whole hallucinogenic motif.
I'm glad we had the chance to share
This time together, kids, that's all there is,
No really, that's all there really is. Nothing
Else on the court docket. Though true, I watched
That raptor soar a while against the setting sun,
A thus far uninhabitable earth-suck of a star
So thank you for inviting me to speak
At your commencement, it's been an honor.
Hook me up with grad parties, text me deets.
If you don't mind, all I've got is this Hazmat suit.

# DEFENSE OF POETRY?

*"...the interlunations of life..."*
—Shelley

Poets are also the unacknowledged contractors
Of the world. Lumber, electrical conduit, pipe,
Sheetrock, track light, double-pane glass.
We are a nation of flaws, here's to
Our foundry fathers. The Laughters of the American
Convolution. The canoes are not really dead,
They're resting. The lake laps against the side
Of the boathouse. Typical canoes. Tyler, too.
Down with slogans, once and for all.
When you find yourself in a poem walking at night
Don't automatically look to the guiltless seas.
This, we have done for centuries.
I have nothing against the ocean, though it seems
To have plenty against me. I refer to my
Astrological sign and the time the tide came up
When I played chess with the cormorants
Stuck out on a prómontóry which is accented on
The first and third syllables, which never feels right,
Does it? Which goes to the general point I'm not
Making. Give me the interlunations of life
Or give me death. One if by hand, two if on
Knees. The people have spoken, we have overheard.
What holds us together is a thread of moonlight.

# THE END OF AN AGE

Goodbye, locomotives and other motives, goodbye.
Moveable type, laptop computers, and quaggas,
Goodbye and goodbye. And goodbye, cantilevered
Bridge, goodbye, my tessellated childhood, bye bye.
Just pretend I know what I'm talking about.
Today, lurchings into reggae's lazy labyrinth,
Tomorrow, videophonic hookup with Tunisia,
Just like that we're surfing jeweled rosewater.
Been working on my theory. Her name is Lucille.
No, that's my guitar, goodbye. My new theory's name
Used to be the Human Genome. The Collected Forays
Of Shakespeare. I want to do with you, I want to do
With you what spring does weakening my knees.
I've consulted this big history of the cinema
And read myself into vacancies the historian left
Vacant, thanks, Historian. One day, Eminem will be
Gregorian chant. Once, there were those
Who believed in the existence of Jean-Paul Sartre.
We keep looking, goodbye, into the moue or the maw
Of the fashion model, assuming hunger would talk back.
No use bringing up when the elephants sang, goodbye.
The dinosaurs were killed by a colossal fiery metaphor,
so long. Online I read they found another dinosaur,
Hello? Today there are more dinosaurs than when I was
But a lad. Anyway, this dinosaur—pterosaur—had a little body
And big wings, making it a constant predator, watch out,

Much like those we dated in our subtracted youth,
So its extinction relates to the rudder that sprouted
Like a caliper from its head, as big as the rest of the bird.
Who can't sympathize? Goodbye, pterosaur, what's your hurry?
I forage in the ash forest seeking a flake
Of snow. I stumble across the anachronistic remote
And change the channels on the horizon.
From this porch of protein I marvel as to how
The streets are all swept clean in the dark.
I tag along with my trusty sidekick, Ciao, Bella.
The sidekicks have bid us all goodnight.

# THE PUNCTUATION OF LIFE

Robins eat fourteen feet of earthworms a day,
I've had a few run-on days like that myself.
Why not hook a fat comma on the recycling bins,
Staple semicolons on telephone poles, air quotes
Around the flight pattern of a mourning dove?
The brace of clouds above cries out for the em dash.
Saint Crispin's Day, I cannot resist the urge
To assassinate the apostrophe. I fumble all night
In bed with a question mark, next morning stagger
On the circumflexed curb, my accent grave and legume.
I'll never again butt into a bar fight between two umlauts.
Please, what brackets you and me apart? Now it feels
Like @ sign six a.m., seems like parenthesis it's June.
Even the finches look exclamation point fatigued.
An avalanche of equal signs when rain falls a vector
On the just and just-so alike. Tuning fork surgically
Hyphenated in my blue-penciled head bullet point. I'm begged
To participate in a phone survey of my national mood.
Takes ten underscore minutes, says he slash she full stop.

# SYMPTOMATOLOGY

Now I'm a joke that works the first time and then
Never again. Can't help that I am ill.
I am sick. Under the weather. Off my feed.
Up to snuff, that's not me. I will never, long as I live,
Lick another handrail or rub my eyes with a chinchilla.
I am a microbial swamp, an airborne tumor,
Not OK, trending poorly. The ski-lift in my eyes
Is out of commission, a long line of miscreants
Waits with tickets to be punched. My hair? It's like that
To cover the surgical scars. Comparatively, scarecrows
Have upside. They said a pet would cheer me up
So I brought home a stray ventilator, now house-trained.
I swallowed a syringe. I devoured small arms fire.
I have a Richter scale attuned along my trigeminal corridor.
I submerged myself in a bath of aftershave
And the tingling sensation reminded me how sick
I am. I need help. I am ill. I'm dabbling in black arts.
Witches, for a good time call. But you leeches, lay off.
Let me be unambiguous. I do not feel at the top of my game.
I am radioactive. I am prehensile, too, let that pass.
My condition is venereal, coronarial, vestigial,
And a little metaphysical, that's just how I am.
I am depressed and repressed, and my immuno-
Deficiency internal combustion engine is
Suppressed. I need to sleep. I need to hit the weights.
Scans reveal I might have experienced at some point

Fetal death. I am a felled tree and an Anglo-Saxon
Poem, I am sick. It was a lousy day when I learned
What goes into head cheese. Not that I need
Your sympathy, spare me. I'm living in a bubble,
Sorry I can't make the party, on account of my
Shingly leaves. It's caused by dirt I ate when I was
An irony-deprived child doing excavation in
The sand box, tra la. My eyes turn bluer by the hour.
There's the matter of an extra arm jutting off:
But it's nice to have back-up when I require
A flashlight to read directions to your house.
I've felt better. There's a spar in my chin, a spike in my toe,
An aquarium of Japanese fighting fish in my gut.
Hard to believe I once knew bliss. Once I pulled a sled
The length of the Iditarod, during the formative college years.
Yes, it's true. Once I even did dressage. This involves
A horse in a shocking way. Once I employed a valet.
He quit. Will you please help? You can't help.

# I WAS JUST LEAVING

Then again, I am always just leaving. It's the best part
Of showing up in the first place. The dog to be fed,
My kid to be picked up at the rink, a trip to pack for,
Anything to obtain clearance from traffic control.
These are not fabrications if somebody believes.
So long has passed since I was just leaving,
I almost forgot I ever arrived. So much ground
We have covered since. We wonder, what if we went
To one school and not another, turned down one street
Where the piano was lifted up the building side,
Missed the connection and the plane went down
In flames. Lives we might have lived, lovers
We might have betrayed or who betrayed us.
Sometimes I'm certain we missed the best times
Somebody might have had. And yet, and yet, who can
Forget the instant anesthesia kicks in—
*Ten, nine,* darkness—or remember it? And then
The black curtain is pulled back and we wake up with
A new knee, or a heart. That time I was just
Leaving was the time I did not, did not pass
By the casement window, descend the marble stairs,
Buttoned up my coat and walked out into the falling snow,
And reached up to pull down my hat against the cold
And realized I'd left my hat upstairs, where I still was.

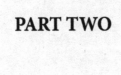

**PART TWO**

PART TWO

# BRIEF BIOGRAPHY OF AN
# IMAGINARY DAUGHTER

*Lonely as my desire is,*
*I have no daughter.*
*I will not die by fire, I*
*shall die by water.*

—James Wright

## #1 [COLLEGE]

We packed your satchel with sweatshirts,
Soccer equipment, and *The Elements of Style*,
Loaded up the Hum Vee, a sad drive to JFK
And the cross-country flight to starting college,
where fortunately due to Advanced Placement
You've already been awarded your MFA
And published your first book.
As we pulled out of the driveway, I slammed
On the brakes, and not on account of Jubilation,
The neighbor's cat. "Stacey," I said, "we have jumped the gun."
"I didn't know we had a gun, Pops," you said.
"This is a figure of speech, a melanophore.
But you can't go to college yet,
Stacey, you're barely by my count five years old."
"That's all right, Daddy-O, nice try.
But my name's not Stacey."

## #2 [PUPPY]

Love this puppy and your love will be repaid.
I can't stress how little this will teach you about life.
Which it will. Which is a lot.
Sometimes, when you're sad, I won't know what to say.
Desire will cut into the bone.
So much we need to cover before you're on your own.
This is a tea kettle, where goldfish won't feel at home.
When I was your age, before you were born,
A war was almost certainly about to break out.
The Russians turned out to be just like us,
Only worse drivers, which is a lot like us, too.
I had a pet once, too, you know. An accordion.
Very tough to train, stained with fluids as it was
About which nothing further need be said.
Your questions matter. No, they really do.
I have no clue as to the white carnations,
No reason to suppose the stars were not meant for you.

## #3 [FISH]

"Do fish sleep?" I am so glad you asked. Once
Upon a time fish did not even catnap.
Childhood has reached a certain point.
More specific than that, I cannot be,

Or less. When you drive to Chartres
You can see it coming at you far away.
Never pass up a cathedral if you can.
Drink lots of water with the strawberries.
Leap before you look too hard, which makes
Things swim in your head, like fish that never sleep.

## #4 [BIRDS...]

"Time's come to talk to you about the birds."
"And the bees?"
"What do you know about the bees?"
"Was just asking."
"A falcon is one bird you can't keep in a cage,
I can't explain why, though I might point
To history for many instructive precedents."
"You have trouble explaining, Dad."
"Anyway, what I like about birds is, they're much
Like dreams—they fly in through a window
Where you didn't know there was a window before."
"I get it. We open to the known and discover
Mysteries left in their place, like putting under the pillow
A tooth that fell out and you come up with the cash
When you need it in the morning, for school."
"Let's stay focused, Amy." "Sure, Reginald."
"I mind it that you call me Reginald, who's he?"
"Someday, Dad, I may fall in love."
"Let's go back to the birds. I don't want to say
Love is for the ornithologists, though such thoughts occur.
Maybe the real topic is experience."
"I knew that." "When?" "You told me." "I never."

"Didn't have to." "That's how, you just know?"
"Life's a vale of tears, Pops, except when it's not."
"Hence, sweetheart, some birds thrive in cages."
"Name three." "I want you to try on some wings.
I want you to take flight. Like the day I gave birth…"
"What?" "The day I gave birth to you was the day of days."
"You feeling OK?" "The epidural worked like a charm,
I felt like I was swimming in air." "I think you're confused."
"I wouldn't be the first, but when they handed you to me
You nursed till you fell asleep." "You're talking about love."
"And some bees sting."

# #5 [BOND]

Once we had a bond, a sacred trust.
I carried you on my shoulders, we watched
The finches dart and feed, I read *The Odyssey*
To you, which OK was a stretch, but who cared
You did not exist? Certainly, not me.
But take the example of Homer.
Would you just give me a chance?
There's an old dog called Argus
Who waits for the hero to show before he dies.
I'm *getting* to the point. If we never had a dog
I would wait for you to arrive from a journey
Forced upon you by chance and fate.
You see, the whole thing's about waiting.
There you are offstage readying yourself
For a grand entrance into a life none of us
Heretofore presumed. I myself ache
Barometrically in concert with the coming storms.

If you never are, I have something left over
Even if it's only me, watching you wade in, as if
You were a great swimmer and this world another shore.

## #6 [SORROW]

*Jamais de la douleur prendras-tu l'habitude.*
*You will never get used to sorrow.*
—Pierre Reverdy

Still, you can practice. Fire trails are good
As are Gothic cathedrals, mid-afternoon.
I say open a special bottle of wine.
I say asseverate by means of a Venetian mask.
When the circus comes to town, take to your bed.
If yours is not available, a friend's may have to do.
You will grow less unaccustomed to sorrow.
What is wrong with that contention? Use
The other side of the page to continue your essay.
The populace is divided, which is why we keep
The populace around. So often it is that we fall in love,
Why don't we just stop? I am thinking of a number
Between one and ten. Correct, the null set.
You can always meet someone at a cafe.
You can always memorize the periodic table.
How can anybody be drowning so far from the sea?
If you come by I'll bake you bread.
If you don't I will hover over the stew.
Vermicular is a word that sounds like what
It is (worms), whereas tumbrel and monger
Not so much. What was it you called to tell me?

# #7 [CAREER]

OK, you want to be a poet, what can I do?
For starters, that's a rhetorical question.
Like when somebody takes the mike and asks,
Do I wake or sleep? Nobody's going to say,
Check aisle five, bulk goods.
Not existing already, you have a leg up.
Poets need emerald green hiking boots,
A complicated country, Chile being a good example,
Red bookshelves, a table cleared largely of
Snow, a badger, a very extensive wine cellar
And a great memory for clouds, streams, death,
Childhood, and dreams. Adopt a little lake,
Keep an eye out for the loons and their advanced
Academic degrees. If somebody comes up to you
After a reading and gives you a telephone number
You have taken a wrong turn. If on the other hand,
Somebody comes up to you, that's pretty good.
And excellent if somebody says, Goodbye, I love you,
I wish you had never been born, which is already
Fortunate as you know for you. And then somebody says,
I'll never write a poem like that if I live to a thousand,
But I'm glad you did, who knows when the plane
Departs, only you should be on board, listening to
The control tower as if these were undecoded secrets
Afloat in the jetstream between your ears. Careful!
Contents in the overhead bin may have shifted.

Finally, when the biographers touch down
And make crop circles, they'll be looking for signs
Of unhappy youth, negligent fathers, insensitive schools.
As if this is news and as if it matters. You're on your own
Here, as you always were and will be.
That's why you wear those emerald green hiking boots
And install the vista where you break the pledge
To settle down by a fire no one will ever douse.

## #8 [GIFT]

I lost the pen you gave me,
The beautiful pen. For hours I overturned
Everything in the house. Nothing, nothing, and nothing
Some more. I called the stores where I shop.
They shared my grief. "I had a Mont Blanc
I lost once myself." This did not speak to my needs.
I looked one last place—your baby album.
There it was, the only thing inside: the pen.
It was almost worth losing it to feel so happy
To find it. Were I a Trappist monk who
Had renounced all earthly possessions
I would not have known such happiness.
It made me drive over to the Golden Gate Bridge
And almost fling myself into my sea.

# #9 [RAIN]

What's in it for you?
On long nights, nothing but that question.
I do love the way the rain falls in June
When it's not supposed to rain.
We could wait in line for sushi or a symphony,
The tire repair, the prescription, or the bridge to reopen.
I want to go to the astronomy museum
And see the cranes nesting in Bolinas.
"A man like me" makes a lot of sense
Only when I do not, which is the case
During equinox, breakfast, and final exams,
Which have all been postponed. What's in it
For you? The sheen on a bird wing at dawn
When the dog is up already barking
Let me out! We stumble down the dark
Searching together for surprises left by the rain.

# #10 [   ]

(Each emptiness yearns to be filled.)

## #11 [CONCEPTION]

When you were conceived and I fell in love
The details need not detain us. Suffice it
To say, a lake may well have been involved.
And the unreliable car. So let me rule out during your
Formative high school years all lakes, all cars.
I'd like to take advantage of
Your never having been born
To remind you that you were
Never less than perfect even if
Imperfectly conceived. Child
Of my bitter old age, child of
My impecunious youth, child
Of refraction, child of prairie,
Wind, will you ever forgive me
For never having been? Will you
Sleep the half-life of swindled
Time and intentional accident?
Think of the rituals we can now
Reinvent. The death of one of us
Is still technically impossible.
Thursday will be our favorite day,
The early summer evening is prime.
I'm going to cook the food
You love, I'm going to read you
A long story for bed,
I'm going to keep my ear
Above your chest the whole night long.

# #12 [HOME]

When I came home you were not there.
At least you're consistent.
I ask the staircase, How was school?
You get the part in the play?
That's nice, I guess I reply to the stairs.
I'm going to paint the whole house
Tonight. Want to help your old dad?
I'll give you time to gather your thoughts,
Wherever you are tonight. Should have left
You dinner for before you met your friends.
Whenever I don't find you, it's not the same.
Maybe we could have watched some TV.
Only I see the set is gone, and in its place,
Is a blue cactus. Also gone, the couch, the chair,
The four walls, and the ceiling,
Which was something I never loved like you.

# #13 [PARADISE]

I'd like to take this opportunity to take
This opportunity to thank you for paradise.
The cars wave their semaphores,
The clouds are milked dry.
I am coming to the place

Where you and I part
For this is something I cannot yet do.
Your room is filled with carolers,
Your closet, with the menagerie.
I'm sending you a card
Postmarked paradise. So you'll know
How to find me, in the wake of the maple trees,
Stuck in the loom of the dark.

## #14 [MEMORY]

"My favorite memory: when you read me
Before bed. I was gifted recognizing the shape
Of letters, not so good, the meaning of words.
Fifty years later, the story remains the same.
I liked the one about the happy dragon,
Almost as much as the sorrowful duck."
"Once upon a time" makes me want you now.
But you're not here and it's not once upon
Anything. I'm working on the e-mail.
Working on the ladder. Working on the bee
That flew into my room. Once upon whenever
I missed you. Thought I saw you
Crossing the tracks near the house,
Carrying a backpack jammed with little dragons.
My own heart is a dragon foraging in a tiny field
Where the other kids break out the bats and gloves,
The cut grass where you lie, unable to wait.
I'm keeping those stories should you decide
To return. I'm learning the rest of my letters,
Stumbling on numbers greater than one.

Love is a fire a dragon brings on,
Love's at the tip of a falcon wing,
Tell me, just once, a story that's for you.

# #15 [TIME]

I'd like to get on your calendar
So pencil in some face time for a few big talks
The books all say we have to have,
If you know what I possibly mean.
The sex talk. The college talk. The driving talk.
I'm sure you'll bring your own questions
To the table, even if we don't happen to own
A single flat surface, but let's not lose sight of
Losing sight of the real conversation.
Which is: I think blue is the best color for you.
I also don't think you're listening to enough music,
Or spending enough time alone in your room.
I wish you would not put all your stuff
Away when you're done or expend energy
Taking out the garbage. I've reassessed
Your dietary revolt: Maybe pizza and fries
Do constitute the perfect nutritional program.
Hope you give Chekov another chance,
He and I would do the same for you.
The report card came home from by the way
The school. I warned you about the trampoline
But I'm not going to go, I told you so.
I see you're excelling in calculus,
Whatever that may be. And the study of ants
And the adjective Byzantine. A chip off

The old block, sweetheart, you surely are not.
Which is why I say blue, kingfisher blue.


## #16 [SISTERS]

A credit card can be useful for restaurants.
No. No, that's what a fork is for.
Remember how I said I would always love
You unconditionally, that nobody would come
Between us? Not even if suddenly you had
A sister? She would be another person
Called a daughter I do not personally have.
Don't get like that, don't, please.
You're still my daughter in a manner of speaking,
One hundred percent. But you made me so happy
I could do with one or two more, and then I went,
One or two? Why not five or six, why not a thousand,
Why not a million more? In China and in India
They leave baby girls on mountain tops all the time.
You see where this is going better than I do,
Who has no clue. Which is what your new sister
Could be saying to you in the night when she shoves
Her way inside and cries, It's me.
And you go, I know, and when you touch her hand
The house turns into a minaret.

## #17 [HISTORY]

Everybody's talking about empire.
Nobody's talking about my nasturtiums.
The candidates were beheaded in the square.
Shun all squares. It's impossible to avoid
Candidates. It is an illusion you were ever alive.
I was never alive, either. Well, there were
A few close calls. I recall the time I rose up
To address the throng and, what to my everlasting surprise
Should appear, hey, no throng. Just me in the place where
A throng is supposed to be. Which is a common
Occurrence as you yourself can testify.
There never is a throng when you need one.
And when you don't, of course, it's there,
As you take strike three, miss the shot,
Hit the wrong note, weep into the cold carrot
Soup. You would have loved my cold
Carrot soup. As a rule, rules are over-
Rated, but when it comes to soup, let her rip.
A soup takes patience. Takes time. You need
Soup to make soup, called stock, so
I'm glad you missed the war. That war
And all the others, too. When it was over
There was a new flag and a cortege,
Men stood on the platform and explained why
The platform would now be demolished.
See what I mean about squares?
I put the ocean outside your door.

Nice ocean, full of fish and water, of course,
Being an ocean. Sometimes, if you look hard,
A ship comes in, your name all over the bow.


# #18 [PLUMS]

Got your note when I woke at noon.
I'm doing more and more these days
Things I do not do. You said you ate the plums
In the ice-box that you believed I was
Probably saving for breakfast. "Forgive me,"
You wrote, "they were delicious, so sweet,
And so cold." Plums, I understand, but
Icebox? Who taught you "icebox"?
Forgot: I rescheduled your checkup
For Tuesday, after school. I don't like
That cough of yours, and let old Doc Williams
Look at the spider bite on your leg.
You could not have enjoyed the plums as much
As I savored your note, which I bet will
One day appear in the *Norton Anthology
Of Notes on Plums.* If I knew where to find you,
I'd plant leaky plum trees you could follow home.
Should have taken another look in that so-called
Icebox. You'd have discovered the Mission Figs,
The Bing cherries, the Fuji apples, the pears,
The peaches, the cantaloupe, and rambutans,
Which look like bristly strawberries
And taste like lychee nuts cross-dressed as almonds.
If you existed I would write you back and tell you
A mouth is a mystery that sometime must be kissed.

Someday you will love someone so hard
Your stomach hurts, like there's a jacaranda
Blooming under your shirt. This is just to say.

# PART THREE

PART THREE

# NEIGHBORHOOD CLEAN-UP ODE:
# THE MUNICIPAL DIRECTIVES

*Do not place anything on top of dilapidated*
*Etruscan plinths.* The waste and detritus
Of the past twelve months: plunked on the curb.
I shove the word "detritus" into a banged-up banana box,
If you haven't used a shirt or idea for a year, toss it now.
I've dispatched the rumpled bed, my college French,
The oceanic color halfway between blue and green.
Ninety percent of the world's population lives one mile
From the shore. Throw this data point away right now.
So there's my expenditure for all to see on the street,
Like red-light window dressing on Amsterdam's quaint
Boulevards. It might be all right, Neighborhood Cleanup,
If I surrender busted books and TVs, and municipal gulls
Flocked and carried each shred of me off into the clouds.
For you have no notion what it was like to be hungover
A sitting duck in LAX and the X disembarks
Before your very bleating eyes, nor do I. But it's so,
And I fold that in bubble wrap, which qualifies as acceptable
Debris. If my door was dead I would hack it in half
Just as you require. Now's the chance to clean up my life.
Today I get rid of 2010, first part of '94, most of '91.
The time I engorged myself on the Nietzschean oeuvre.
The authentic shades of love, dried up house paint
In the can, an environmental hazard of the second degree.
Old instruments, begone—shepherd's crook, zither, stethoscope.
Things I don't need, things I let go, things someone please steal,

Only one thing's left won't let go of me: how loss is loss
Is loss is loss is loss is loss is loss.

# THE SATRAP WILL SEE YOU NOW

Because later he has a tennis date.
He'd delight in a bowl of figs,
Your fatted calf, a bucket of balls.
These days, he likes a little company.
Take a shot if you can tell a joke.
The loneliness of a satrap is the hood
On his falcon, a goat on the side of a hill.
When he graduated first in his class
From Satrap School, was he a tent on fire!
Taxes to levy, rebellions to crush,
Aspiring maidens to bed.
They would feed him grapes, he'd shave
Their legs. He updated his threaded-gold
Caftans, he encrusted his shoes with gems.
Satrapping around took its toll in time.
His memoirs did not take off.
Nobody in Hollywood took his call.
Take the Satrap to Work Day was a bust.
Edicts were ignored, decrees, mocked.
He begged the dog to chase the ball.
The Saluki preferred the rabbit dream.
The Satrap will see you now,
Tomorrow he beheads himself in the square.

# WEDDING SEASON

The bride was Spring Break and the groom was called
Google.com. To the rotunda top rockets white doves,
Down go the Jell-O shots, Irish, and rum.
Desire wed Sincerity—who could see that coming?
And what a surprise, Cricket and Hummingbird.
Who would have counted on the hundred-strong
Harmonica marching band? Nucleotide and Glowworm.
Stock Option and Periodic Table. Precambrian Era
And Harley Davidson. Ship of Fools and In a Station
Of the Metro. Breast Stroke and Anterior Cruciate
Ligament. War of 1812 and Sonnet 129.
True, some pairings seemed inevitable.
Scar and Veil. Jealousy and Virgin. Tuna and Rye.
Spa Music and Deep Tissue Thai Massage.
Maine Lobster and Drawn Butter sent a save-the-date.
It was sad when Muse thwarted Poetry on the pyre.
Heartbreaking when Great White and Moonwalk
Flipped over the buffet and turned backs on in-laws.
But nothing rivals when Irony cheated on Post-
Modern as hip hop kicked in at the champagne bash.
Live long enough, and see? Sunday Brunch married
Gettysburg Address. I thought she appeared pale
And he'd prove nothing but a rant,
But look—I was wrong, I'll be going to the bris.
I've RSVP'd already to the wedding of
Middle East Conflict and Great Barrier Reef.

Something about weddings makes me want to
Plunge headlong into a tiered butter cream cake,
Entrust my car keys to the drunk valet.

# EMPEROR WITH NO CLOTHES

*If you care about yourself at all, come to your own aid while there's still time.*
—Marcus Aurelius 3.14

Citizen of Rome, you are the center of the universe.
Problem is, circumference is—take a guess—me.

"Some things are impatient to be born
While others are impatient to die." Don't say

I did not warn you. Next time they swear
Shit happens, pop them square in the nose.

This will not help anybody, but helping is
The farthest thing from my imperial mind.

If you keep your spirit blameless and pure
People will drape you with laurels but

No one will have sex with you in backseats
Or marble mausoleums or anywhere else,

A small price to pay for honor and respect
Though not for me, being an emperor with no clothes.

Just pretend today is the last day of your life
And act accordingly—not that such strictures

Apply to Yours Truly, sports fans.
The forces of evil march on the fortress

Of your self. I wish I could explain why.
But what if evil did not exist and what if

Your self was no fortress, see what I mean?
Stoics get a bad name. *Not in touch with feelings.*

*Too rigid. Know-it-all cocksure mothers.*
So the Stoics retain PR firms, don't tell a soul.

If you really knew what was good for you,
And you do, why do you care I'll flay you alive?

True, pissing off your emperor is a poor plan,
Even one like me mounted bare-assed on a steed.

Once upon a time, children... The story peters out.
Circus revels and gladiatorial raves—

Seen one, seen them all. Life is tiresome,
When will it end and will we ever notice?

I wish I knew. Really, I wish I cared.
My pal, Marcus Aurelius, natters day and night:

"Living is more like wrestling than dancing."
Guess he never saw me take Molly at the club.

And he says we always have the option of
Having no opinion. Right. Like he knows.

OK, then, where did I put my pants?

# TALK

Thank you for coming tonight. Like you
I tried to get out of it, but look,
Here we all are—well, those of you who
Aren't still killing time in the lobby
Hoping for a small earthquake,
Which, to be honest, I understand.
After I speak I will take your questions.
I bet they will be great questions,
I bet some of them will have already
Appeared in print, I bet you will
Dedicate your question to your spouse,
I bet I will disappoint one and all
But I promise afterward good wine.
You know how you're driving cross country
And you just mainlined a pot of bad
Coffee at the truck stop and you must get
To the coast in time for a father's funeral
That takes place in two days and gas is on F
And driver is on E? And the highway lines
Undulate like the *sine* function in trig class?
Well, my talk will be full of images like
That, you just wait and see. I will read
Selected passages, please turn off your phones.
At the reception you may possibly conclude
If they invited me to speak there's hope
For you—or maybe just the opposite.

You are in luck because: no PowerPoint
In my bag of tricks. A, that's so Two
Point Oh. Second, I haven't a clue.
I will lighten the mood from time to time
With anecdotes and self-depreciating jokes
That amount to humble brag, which you'll
Sniff out, if you ever come in from the lobby.
There are still spots open at the front.
They asked me to talk about the new book.
If I could talk about it I would not have
Written it. We all know people who go on
And on about books they are writing and do not
Manage to write them. OK, that last point
Makes me sound like a jerk and my goal
Is you don't find that out first. Be on
The lookout for literary allusions and influences.
Later please tell me what they are, thanks.
But you'll probably ooh and ah about
The cowboy shirt and alligator boots—
Sorry, Ecosystem. Those of you in the lobby,
It's lovely up here behind the podium.
I have no idea how they will introduce me,
Someone, they'll say, who needs no introduction.
When I finish, books will be for sale, guess where?
In the crowded lobby. Unless the arsonists succeed.
One of you may find yourself I guess
Strangely smitten. Talks are where I met
All my exes, none of whom could attend
Tonight. Though I could, as you plainly see.
Now it's time to begin, then it will be time
For regrets. Next time, I promise to be better.

# OBSERVATIONS OF A FAILED THERAPIST

Hold on there, girlfriend, we don't talk like that
In here. Your loving mother had her reasons,
That's my analysis. So let's try again, shall we?
This time without the self-pleading, the injured
Merit, which is my patented personal go-to move.
Your world is full of contradictions? What was
Your first clue, Ms. Assistant Professor?
Oh, mortality, that is a bitch. Let's circle back
To something you mentioned, how you loathe me,
How I am a voyeur and a narcissist both.
I saw that coming, I didn't go to shrink school
For my health, you know. The technical term for your
Problem is transference, so it's predictable
For me to be loathed. And what *about* my scarf?
I have it on good authority it works with my complexion.
Perhaps seeing a female therapist *would* be indicated.
But I was thinking canine. I was thinking gnome.
It's all about you, isn't it, young lady,
And your precious crises, what about me?
A man has feelings, a man's going to die, too,
You know. A man can't always account for his
Whereabouts, his overriding despair and uselessness.
I see our time is up. Our time's been up since
You first showed up in black boots and weeping.
No, please don't go. I'd like you to close
Your sea green eyes and free-associate a while.

"Pathetic" is not an appropriate response. Has
Consideration been given to pharmaceuticals?
To even out my swings of mood.
I'm not ruling out brain surgery, I'm not
Discounting a career shift. Only thing in the way,
I'm just not sure you're ready to change.
Had this dream about you the other night.
We were in the choir loft and the water
Level was rising and rising and you spoke
To me in I think German, which normally
I don't understand and where were we going just now?

# HEAR YE, HEAR YE, LISTEN UP

During the great syncopation of King Mope Mope,
In the reign of the Cruciferous and Crustaceans,
The heyday of the Ho-ho and the year of the Pot Belly Pig,
There came to be either a census or consensus
When the moon waxed and waned above taffied templates
That had pillared us, pondered us, and pitied us,
In no particular disorder. A time of war it was
Like any old time at all. The people,
They gathered as people do in defiance of edicts
And of Dame Edith, who refused placation and oral
Surgery despite the delineated protocols.
When the sun fell into the sea, during the surge
Of the flippered and the flippage of the Megatots,
The tetrarch Manuel bullwhipped the oligarch
Oswald, who was used to such cowtowing by
The rashly incipient. Still, the word came down,
The marker was called, the field was plowed,
And thus it was that Philia's countenance shone
Upon the multitudes, who obviated it not.
Woe betimes, snipped the intubating respirators,
And a proclamation went out to all the outlier regions,
Ruled by the Regicides, potentates of possibility.
The voice of one lying in the wilderness:
Behold, the hour is come, the nigh is near.
Behold, all is forgotten but not forgiven,
The crooked is made straight, but straight

Has been tempered by a million fires stoked
In the belly of nought in the desert ops of cluelessness.
All would be made clear, all would become new,
Now that time had been dunked into a cold bath
And one may walk alone, shedding raiments
Like failed fashion hypotheses for the runways of Fall.
Take heed, for the lions, the vipers, the wolves
Are suppurating in the plazas of continuity.
That sense of expectation billowing within like the wind,
That is the conviction you have lived,
That despite all the evidence, you must go on
For a while longer, until the winnowing fork
Breaks on your tongue and the granary seeds
Scatter like so many beplunked notes.
Hear ye, listen up, this is the word from on high:
You must perforce gather your possessions
Along with loved ones and cross the closest river.
You don't have to be a loser in order to be found.
You don't need to be heard in order to cry for help.
You must be contemporaneous, though, to live.
Ascend the next mountain and suck in all the air.

# MY CONTRIBUTOR'S NOTES

*Awards*

Heterosexual Agenda Male Bias Runner-up.
Agronsky Wetlands Chapbook Champ.
Bicameral Grant for Sidereal Studies.
Honorable Mention Dissociated Poets Prize.

*Education*

Went ten rounds with a liposuctioned trombone,
Which is what I get for leading the marching band
Through Malibu. Memories of birth trauma and marriage
Turn crisper year by year, and I spun
A mean plate at my summer carnival internship.
Somewhere I've got *magna cum nada* degrees
And crop circles, several leading Rockies,
The Houston Skyline and one half of Brooklyn.

*Publications*

My poetry has been tarred and minimally
Feathered, and I plagiarized the change jar
For beer after the off-campus reading last week.
Can't explain why teachers took a pass
On the resume or why my long-delayed manuscript
Was barbecued to cinders in what investigators
Determined to be auspicious circumstances.
If only editors could read me. I will go on. They told me to.
Here's something almost considered by *Sports Illustrated*:

"My Love Life"
The NCAA tournament brackets have been at last
Announced. I'm looking for an underdog
To come through. A point guard
Who can set the tempo, who can make a mid-range
Jump shot, a coach who's good drawing X's and O's,
Schooling the zone, and employing clichés.
All right, one time, she lost the handcuff keys.
Another time misplaced the egg beater,
Took a flyer on the French drain ooh la lah.
Basketball is a team game, it's about moving without
The ball, playing defense with her gorgeous feet,
About playing your game, staying within yourself
And sometimes within somebody else. Get an opening,
Go for the hoop. Take what the opposition gives you
And don't give it back. Some very good teams
Are always left out of the tournament, very hard
To say why. Basketball was invented in 1891
By James Naismith, a Canadian with two peach baskets
And thirteen rules. He wanted boys to have something
To do indoors during the long, long winter months.

Current Project
Inventing new sex games that do not require
Abject pleading. Otherwise, a spider took up
Residence in the corner. When the sun pours in
And the wind picks up, filaments glow like neon.
Please find attached said spider web.

# THINGS I NEVER SAID I SAID

I never said elephants sing when they mourn
Though I could have because it's true.
I never said scars would one day heal
Because how would somebody like me know?
I never really said I took your cumin,
Never said it looks like rain, wear a coat.
I never said I'd water your house plants
When you ran off to Mexico without me.
That I knew what you were going through,
Which's what *you* said to me, and maybe
It's the case I never said I'll never go to
The movies ever again or iron my white shirt
But I did say I stole your caraway seed,
Which you didn't even know you owned,
Which speaks volumes, yet another thing
I never said I said. You could write a book
On all the things I never said I said,
And I never said that, either.
I never said the gas tank was full
And the yogurt was still good despite
The expiration date, never once said
I'd prefer cremation someday or possibly
Ever, that I was fixated upon death,
No, because that was you now in Mexico
Without your lonely house plants. Did not
Say I was falling in love with you,

Because I already had. That I'd bring home
Thai takeout, the pad Thai you love
Unlike me—you know what I mean—even when
I do not say what I never said I said. Never
Said I was a good dancer, either, never said
Sorry about that party, that I put my hand
On your friend's knee, except for one time.
And about losing your shoes at the wedding:
They were fantastic shoes and your feet
Looked so gorgeous enwrapped by those black
Straplets, but, being an idiot, missed my chance,
Which I never said I said, and you took them off,
A hot night in the Valley, and we all danced
Till I forgot I was dancing, more like breathing
Inside your lungs, which was the main thing
I never said I said because I couldn't believe that
Was the end of us, that night when your shoes
Disappeared. I never said I said I hated Mexico.
I never said I'm returning the cumin, but I did,
That I've watered your parched plants, so I'm
Saying them now, things I never said I said.

# THE BAR AT THE END OF SOME OTHER ROAD

Kind of place nobody's ever walked in for the soup.
You order the soup. Barkeep thinks he's famous and has
Bottle caps for eyelids and a girlfriend who cuts
His hair so when track lights flick, looks like
Broken glass rained on his head.

Place where it feels like a fight's always about to
Break out and you're in the middle.
Combustion, then silence oomphs like a blanket over a fire,
*Boom* from the back room like a flat tire, you doing eighty.
Kind of place lobster traps give up, hang a hundred miles
From the sea on the cork ceiling, fish nets limp on the walls.
If you stare too long at the baseball game on TV
You might go blind, a risk you'll have to take.

Where nobody talks to you and when they do
They stare straight ahead, like now with this girl,
Can't tell for sure if she's pretty or a girl, and she goes,
You new in town? Like she means it. Says
She's never seen you in here, which is
One true thing you both have in common.

Kind of place a girl like that gives you her name
And wind picks up and you see corn silos for days
And trucks, and dogs that would drag her out of
A burning car if they have to, which you can understand,

You might do the same, the least you could do. Now her name
Comes back: Elaine. Definitely rhymes with *Elaine*.

She asks who's winning. She means the game, but
You know better. The pearlescent white
Buttons on her cowboy shirt gleam like her perfect teeth,
The one thing perfect in this kind of place,
Where a bowl of soup is nothing you should count on.

# READ DIRECTIONS FIRST

Don't palpate ambivalent tangerines or breasts.
This just looks like an exit. Allow one minute to cool.
Three nasal applications under waterfall
Max daily. After opening, refrigerate.
Upon closing, oscillate. Refrain from
Checking tire pressure while operating vehicle,
Which may prove unsafe under certain
Conditions. Solving for X, don't forget Y.
Safety glasses advised. Nobody without hard hat
Allowed on work site. Shake well.
Pour carefully. Sing desperately. Wash before
Wearing in cold water with colors you like.
Elevate the legs, apply polar icecap melt.
Decant over candle, sauté till translucent.
Have a problem? Contact Customer Control.
When oxygen mask drops, there is not time
To answer the CEO's urgent sext message.
Put your tray in an upright locked position.
Levitate like this. Leave firearms at front desk.
Treat a corner of fabric first. Never
Connect ground wire during tsunami.
Restrict usage to daylight hours.
Wait while I check your account, this
May take a few seconds. In the meantime,
Hold on, could be your day. *That?* Nothing to fear,
Just somebody's lame idea for Halloween.

Forget your password? Check back Christmas.
Don't stick anything in my ear unless you mean it.

## NO ANIMALS WERE HARMED IN THE MAKING OF
## THIS POEM

Though llamas gobbled up the rhymes
And the camel spit on the box of ghazals.
Polar bear extras were fitted with cross-country skis
While seal pups splashed inside a wheezy villanelle.
And as for the great white sharks, I forced
Them to attend the dolphin relief benefit.
Horses mingled on the mesa with the surly unicorn
Without incident, and the black mambas
In economy were issued temporary library cards.
The chimpanzee unfortunately was pulled over,
Driving through a yield sign and cited for
Transporting barbarically yawping macaws
Whose Tourette's syndrome negatively impacted
The highway patrol officer. Meanwhile,
Lions balked about pilates classes required
By the code but the juggler did employ stunt
Doubles when working with the condor eggs.
Despite rush hour traffic the alligators crossed
The interstate and tickled the ear of the Jack Russell
Comatose on the veranda. I'm happy to report
Bunnies were cuddled by raccoons for a change.
When the Cooper's hawk shilling computer sales
Knocked on the cyberdoor with additional memory
Uploads, this came in handy, and when the tarantula
Pouted we needed stories to tell round the ol' campfire.
Now, I do need to concede humans were dinged up

In the making of this poem. A B-lister
On the lam smoked a baggie of speed-laced weed
And kissed the starlet till her lips glowed and glowed.

# THE OBSESSIVE-COMPULSIVE ATTENDS
# A COSTUME PARTY

With a turtle in my soup and a pill on my tongue,
With a beer in my scrubbed paw and a comet
In my urinary tract, with a cowboy hat on top
Of my conditioned head and a car that never starts up,
I left notes for the house sitter, just in case.

If the Pretty Jessica rosebush should bloom
While I'm gone, no need to panic and compose some ode.
PJ plays her little games, but keep an eye on that
Wily wisteria, which I just don't trust. If the rescue
Dogs whine, give them Critique of Pure Reason.

Let's say the jazz quartet mold in the cellar
Jams all night with sump pump and sheer walls.
Let's say the water pipes freeze and burst.
Let's say the street roils with a seven point one.
Let's say the Huns solicit for Vandal relief.

What if aliens near the barbeque pit descend?
Could be the night of the lunar eclipse,
Could be I'm registered to vote on nuclear waste,
Could be the fireplace glow won't die down,
Could be darkness falls like fruit from the trees.

Feel free to sit in any of the vanquished chairs,
To stock the cupboards with psycho-pharmaceuticals.

You can use the sheets, towels, and barbells,
But I wish you'd please keep out of my dreams.
I will be returning around the crack of dawn.

Don't smack the man in a cowboy shirt with
The cast-iron frying pan, try the tambourine.

# SOMEDAY I'LL GO BACK

Someday I'll go back someday
When no one's watching who cares,
Where the bike'll be chained outside
The ER someday. Somebody should
Go back, I still have the blue scrubs,
After I work up a good sweat
At the gym soon as the movie's over.
I'll go back someday first thing
After I rehang the door,
Patch the holes in the walls.
That's when I'll go back,
When we got the dog at the pound
Before the asteroid shoved
The earth off its axis, blocked
The sun and dinosaurs blinked,
Before fish sauntered from the sea,
Back when docs smoked before
9/11 and the Gettysburg Address.
I'll go back someday, someday I hope
Someday, after rivers overflowed
And fires jumped the line I'll go back,
After the flyover and the drone drive by.
Someday I'll find the sparrow
That crashed into the window,
Lift it up and it will fly off, then
Someday I'll go back someday

When it's long after last call,
When if anybody has cause
Speak now or forever hold
Your peace, back to the time
When the stands were packed
And I threw the perfect pitch
In my mind and I'll go back.
I want to go back someday
Where babies come from someday
How penicillin was discovered
And the lost city of Atlantic
City, let me go back to where
I left my luggage and my keys
Which I never need now that
I need to go back the day someday
You asked, "Where'd you get the car?"
And I went, "From the shop," and you said.
"OK don't tell me," and I said, "Fine."
Let me go back when we drove
Till you glimpsed a lake below
And then you jumped out, undressed
At the water's edge and dove in
And it was dusk and you swam
Alone and I waited in the car
And I was the one submerged.
Someday I wish I could go back
To when trees riffled with your laugh
Looming over the lake, lucky lake,
And immersed you and also me
Someday I'll go back someday,
And find you onshore as if I'd
Never gone, then someday I'll go back
Someday back before this all began

When I'll go back someday, someday.
I'll go back someday, unlock
Your bike and ride away, away,
Someday, which is what I'll do
When someday I come back, someday.

# HEDONIC ADAPTATION

A boy's first fifty years are quite precious.
I cannot stress enough how crucial Puccini
And the overhand curveball can be. That way
His knees won't buckle during *La Bohème*
When a curve ball starts out from behind his ear.
His first five decades of life can be pivotal.
Introduce him to the pleasures of the dunes,
The combustion engine, oh, and parabolas, too.
Give him names for birds and dreams of flight.
Show him death's card tricks so he won't be
Suckered though he will be which is why you do.
Teach him what money can't buy—both things.
Researchers confirm the theory, they ran tests.
They put the 40-year-olds in a canary cage,
The 30-year-olds on a South Seas atoll,
The 20-year-olds inside the computer's cloud,
The 10-year-olds in a kingdom by the sea.
Lab coats said dare to eat a peach. 'Tis not
Too late to seek a newer world and leafy greens,
To ruffle fringed epaulets in the marching band.
No need to join the men's reading group or build
A summer retreat, but I do think his hothouse
Orchids could stand a tweak and his dogs would like
To lie 'round a fire with him when he cracks the spine
Of a Jean Jacques Rousseau. Nothing finer than bow
And arrow on the fjords, a breakfast of shirred eggs

With a dollop of golden caviar. Timing, you roustabout,
Timing. Draw not to an inside straight. Sleep not
In a seal pup's skin. Breathe not one word of golf.

# ANTHRO APOLOGY FIELD NOTES

*"I hate traveling and explorers."*
—*Claude Lévi-Strauss,* Tristes Tropiques

We fail when we bring preconceptions as to the primitive
Mind, or assume ours isn't.
                              If I may continue.
Even so, for me, once is enough with a meal of bugs
In batter fried to a golden crisp. I prefer my bugs
Where they used to be in the jungle, sipping on my eyes,
Twisting parasitically in my ethnographer's guts.
Here they venerate vodka and Converse High Tops,
Tie garlands on crutches, put on crash helmets for bed.
Have stumbled on no arrowheads, bowl shards, or bones,
But note how dejected all their cars appear,
Like Russian kitchen appliances (sketches attached).
Their sex lives are rich with play and assault and battery,
And during early onset puberty, boys and girls could be heard
Once night fell in the forests, clicking their helmets.
I'd heard accounts of cannibalism but could not confirm
If they roasted or boiled or ran each other through a juicer,
Which is a controversial means of obtaining nutrients.
On every corner, chickens, pigs, goats, and ideas
Are being sacrificed to their gods, of which there are many,
None of whom have names that can be pronounced
Though all resemble armadillos with anteater tongues.
The females universally menstruate on the same night,
Which is when males run like Pamplona into the stadium,

Passions running high over the national sport,
Which, near as I can tell, is collective amnesia.
This extraordinary tribe cries out for more research
But it will not be completed by me, as here I've made
My new home. Once I heard the nuclear-collider-size
National tea kettle go off, signaling the incursion of
Enemy bands, who seized the movie houses first,
Then fell asleep during trailers, woke up and slinked
Back, popcorn in their beards, across the border. The whole
Country has one telephone, and when I picked up
It was always my ex, and her song was the same:
Wash off the face paint, unplug the nose and ear posts,
And return. Last night I heard the communal orchestra
Of metronomes, tuning forks, and freight trains
And caught myself yearning for somebody to show up quick
With the cracked ice and High Tops but not my ex.
The volcano is due to blow, I can feel it, my only refuge
The salty sea, my crash helmet, and my notes from the field.

# BEETHOVEN'S, FIFTH, SAN, FRANCISCO,

It was raining paisley umbrellas and we kept
Bumping into them on the swarmed sidewalks.
Most times I go to the symphony hall
Somebody just nods off and snores
Till he's poked in the ribs. Hope tonight
That promises not to be me. The 19th century
Is a very important century for music,
Factories, and novels that go on and on.
You think when Beethoven sat down at
The piano he was thinking 21st century?
I myself have been known to approach
An unsuspecting piano, the mood hits and night
Is coalescing around a few precious concepts
Too transparent to be delineated by such an
Unreliable aviator. Beethoven may have been
Insane, but then again that was so 19th century.
Dostoevski, etc. And let's not forget Nietzsche.
What always gets to me in the Fifth is
The sneaky melody line, the lilt in the air, a light beam,
How a field opens, like with too much moonlight
And pixillated pixels birthday-caking about
And moonlight is something of which
You can never have enough. When I
Was in school, it was considered bad form
To write a poem about a piece of music.
I still inscribe to this theory, though now I dispute

The word "about" in the phrase "about a piece
Of music," and now that I think about it,
Also "piece." "I find it pointless,"
Writes Igor Stravinsky, "and dangerous to over-
Refine techniques of discovery" in his book
*Poetics of Music,* which if you don't know
Stravinksy the way I don't know Stravinsky
You'd find hard to believe. Now the second
Movement of Beethoven's Fifth is really
Lush. I hate the word "lush" for reasons
Too belabored to be obvious. It's enough to
Make me leap to my feet and forget about
My colonoscopy, about which I pledge to add
Nothing further. Beethoven's almost too beautiful
To hear is what I'm trying to get around
Saying, but I'm still tracking down that part in
Stravinsky, and I'm giving up, hearing the oboes
And the strings call out, and I'm going with them,
And sure enough, somebody's snoring, but
At least it's not me with tight shoes kicked off.
In the 5th Symphony Beethoven gives us
A space to step back and wander alongside,
Figuring out what we are doing where we are,
And then, wham, back to melody and ta ta ta
TA!, electric wavelets on the brain's craggy shore,
I just can't get it, I don't know what to say
Except time speeds up not in a bad way like
Brennan's Bar, closing time, but in a we-got-next-
Game kind of way when we know we have the right
Mix of inside/outside. See what happens when the bird cage
Door flings open? That's the Fifth for you.

# DEEPAK AND SECRETS OF THE UNIVERSE

Deepak and I were flapping our gums about secrets
Of the universe. He's a guru, he thinks that gives him
A right. Actually it was more about the beer.
He was talking hops, he was talking water quality,
But the game was on TV so I'm not totally sure.
He was not the easiest roommate, as you'd expect.
Gurus don't wash their dishes or take out garbage,
They steal your shirts and girlfriends and later go,
"Was that your shirt or girlfriend? Sorry, man."
He's probably levitating somewhere by a hot spring
Now and I don't miss my shirts or girlfriends
As much as I miss him. Deepak taught me a lot.
Like, peeling a hard-boiled egg requires
Spiritual discipline, hand-eye coordination,
And having a hard-boiled egg. Time was,
My universe was devoid of eggs and purpose.
I don't like going to New Year's Eve parties
Anymore, especially those I'm not invited to.
The fancy parties feature bubbly and caviar,
Which is sturgeon eggs, served with chopped
Onion and still more eggs, so no thanks,
I've had my fill. Think I'll watch the ball
Drop at midnight if I don't fall asleep
First in Times Square on my television.
My planetarium tells me the universe
Is a scrum of stars and is rowdy as

Texas when I run out of gas and conviction
On a dark desert road in the middle of winter.
Once people thought there was music made by
The spheres, a calliope before iTunes and Spotify.
One thing you can count on with this universe—
Cherry-picking your friends, stupid universe,
Turning them into dust and decomposing memories.
Here's my hat, universe, what's your hurry?
You shouldn't eat a plate of hard-boiled eggs
At a single setting, the least of my problems.
The most of my problems: the racket above,
Furniture being rearranged by the insomniacs
Upstairs, like they can't wait for sunrise,
Which I get, what's the use waiting on this universe?
Deepak, I'm tired of this tired universe and its laws,
Its nasty little secrets, same jokes it does not know
How to tell, how my energy is hardly conserved,
How entropy possesses a primitive appeal.
I was wondering if you'll ever come back, pay the rent,
Pick up the belongings you left behind. Then I looked
In your boxes, saw all of my stuff was yours.

# MY MISSION STATEMENT

*"To bring inspiration and innovation to every athlete in the world."*
—Nike Mission Statement

My mission is to be a unique driving experience.
My mission is to be putty in your hands.
My mission is to be your favorite pair of jeans.
My mission is to whisper in your ear in
Several preselected Romance languages. To star
In a movie that takes Sundance by storm.
(I hope Penelope Cruz will be in it
Even though she will contractually throw pans
Of ink on my head and shoot me colorfully
With a sleepy pistol and make her lips do that
Pouty thing upon which we can hang
*The Collected Works of Henry James*.)
Which reminds me. My mission is
To rewrite the dull parts of the *Kama Sutra*.
Because, listen, people! What's a man without a dream?
I say he's calamari soup. I say he's a man without
A mission statement. This is why my mission
Is to be a global partner and a preferred
Provider. To serve nutritious food to
A hungry world. To leave it all on the field,
To go hard when coach calls my number.
My mission is to write one thing you must
Slip under your pillow. My mission is:
Be the pillow. My mission is: Be the night.

My mission is to bring inspiration and innovation
To each recluse in town, to every space
Station captain, to all radio listeners too shy
To call in, to even the stranger who left a nice note
On my windshield that time. You know who you are.
My mission is, be in business forever.

# POEMS IN WHICH

**Write the vision:**
**Make it plain on tablets**
**so that a runner may read it.**

**Habakkuk 2:2**


**I got up early Sunday morning**
**because it occurred to me that the word**
*which*
**might have come from a combination of** *who* **and**
*each*

**Ron Padgett**

I

## Poem in which he sets up shop:

How do you *think* the pearl got its big break?
First it was shy, loath to forsake a shell so sweet and Polynesian,
and next thing you know, it's a Nieman Marcus frontispiece.
As for me, I've figured out prices but not yet services
I should render. This will come in time, with the first thaw,
with a crate shipped from the Andes or the wonton soup
from downstairs. Things could be tough at first, consider
the competition, which is cut-throat and predacious
and looks a lot like the ex would after sex-change surgery.
I've got to avoid acrimony, which consumers sense.
They catch a whiff of a fire sale and you're dead meat.
Speaking of sex, should I patent that position that makes
them claw at the ceiling in dreams I wish won't stop?
I will accept credit cards, personal checks, scruples,
and splinters off the Holy Rood. My calls may be
monitored for customer satisfaction, their joy is
my number two priority, select the menu that most closely
applies. We can schedule a photo shoot once
I determine what to do with my hands, now that pipes
are passé along with tweed and canonical elbow patches.
Vulnerability pays big, so I should be caught
cuddling with a banjo or strumming a little llama.
The complications of setting up shop—you have no idea.
I say offer something that can't be done without.
A good marching song. An explanation of evil. Maps of
a silver mine and a testy caged canary. Stronger iamb, slinkier simile,

thousand-watt testimonial to wilt convention carnations.
I'll get a website, my own venture-capitalist, iron-clad
contracts, and copyright the cassoulet. When I go public
my price-to-earnings ratio will bloom like the wisteria
and off the satellites birds will bounce their psalms.

## Poem in which he gives precise directions how to get there:

You'll find it steamy among the courtly Cape Buffalo.
Their conservative political positions are entrenched,
so don't bring up the vegetarianism topic unless
you have time to kill. Now, then, just beyond
the clearing you will enter a restaurant walk-in
refrigerator. A lovely word for what the sun does
going silver is *argentine*. There will be a sign saying
"The Argentine." Go there only if you like
show tunes. Anyway, that's a moat complete with raft.
Paddle, Huck, honey, to the blue island and hunker
down for a good seven years. Write your memoirs,
which are big these days, and wag a magisterial finger.
Master the isle's local tongue. That done,
critique the isms, give to the march of paradigms,
build a mound in the shape of your phallus,
or, if yours is not handy, any available phallus.
Merge with your mother the sea, your sister the moon,
your best friend in high school the weight room.
When you wash ashore, say hello to Nebraska.
Of course, you'll be in Minsk. That's why I'd like,
if I may, to impart some advice I heard that meant
a lot to me when I was refusing to grow up:
Go deep. Move fast. Keep low. Aim high.
(Or was it, Go fast, move deep, aim low, keep high?)
Just pay no attention to the harmless harpies. If you're
quiet the griffons will gently light on your occiput.

Step carefully around the icons, taste the indigenous
cornucopias, watch out for the shadowy harbingers.
A man will be leaning against a buckeye tree
offering you a kiss. Do what you have to do.
A woman says her breasts are tender, would you stop?
Here's where things get banal: As you drive
through the millennium you'll notice it's quiet
in the hive for this time of night. One more thing,
about the dark thoughts you are beginning to have:
You're almost there. All that's left is to slip on
your headphones and shift into the next worthy gear.

## Poem in which no one appears to show up for his party:

The clean-up committee seemed elated,
and so were the old friends who could
never talk heart-to-heart during parties.
Amaryllis and periwinkle, everywhere
birds of paradise, and the not bad
champagne chilled down, and before
I knew it, no one showed. This was good
I guess for someone's grandfather who
post-surgery would have laughed too hard
and the big guy I never would invite
who leaks out tears near the fireplace,
the incredible comeback and drive into
the power pole. At least you-know-who's
husband didn't challenge the whole room
to arm wrestle and didn't get caught
in the sauna with you-can't-be-serious.
At least what's-her-name (black clunky
shoes, black turtleneck, black garrotted hair),
didn't read *The Idiot* sprawled on the love seat.
At least no one fed the Japanese fighting fish
pâté. And no one had the bright idea
of introducing the rottweiler to the toucan.
The whole night, not a whisper of *Tarantino*.
Nice that pillows won't lounge on the lawn,
that no trembling earring washes out to sea.
And good thing the paparazzi will be out of sight

when I turn into the life of my own party
and the wallflower sweeps me off my feet.

## Poem in which he shares what he learned today at the spa:

I should take better care of my biggest organ,
says The Spa News, and they mean my skin. Were
you aware that you shed 5 billion dead skin cells
a day? That dead skin accounts for 80% of household dust?
If you're anything like me, you won't put off hiring
that domestic help. In the spa I also learned, from
watching the younger smooth organs pass me by,
how to grow old gracelessly. In addition, you have
28 thousand pressure points and 72 channels or so
for chi, that the state of California considers my diet
a class B felony. As I wait here in my plush terry
robe and smart red rubber espadrilles, I would not
dream of telling alien abductors where
to harvest, but here's got to be more fertile
than Roswell, New Mexico. Today I found out, too,
that I do not technically need sex to survive,
though it may in fact need me. Have I mentioned,
not to brag, that my second biggest organ is my
linch pin, my third my thalweg—or is it my lunette?
Did you know that when I am in love my biggest organ
sings, that the air tastes sweet, that your name
is a lozenge down the slide of my throat?
I was all primed for the herbal body wrap (though
it was not rosemary and thyme), and up pops the potpourri
migraine again. Which is when it dawned that I too

will someday die and that deluxe spa packages
would not be ill-advised. No wonder on this slick
of ointment all I want for lunch is extra salt
with my six margaritas. Pry from my face the cucumber
wedges, let me and my supple nib breathe.

## Poem in which he demonstrates your influence upon his life:

I hereby take the city of Chicago and rename it for you.
It was nothing, but you're welcome. Next stop, Minneapolis.
You know, string theory experts, even those ejected from
the ballgame for entering the field of play, opine that six extra
dimensions curl and loop around the staid old ones
we drolly take to the bank—length, depth, breadth,
and miasma. One of these dimensions circulates
you, beyond the bending, the aftershocked echo.
That's where I marvel over the striated sheen of lake
while I'm squinting into the brash matutinal sun.
Remember? How I used to hate change?
Not that kind—coins. Anyway, I'm cooking up a batch
of tender imprinted with the fulgency of your lips.
Keeps me busy till I come up with a name for Cleveland.
Thanks to you, we can cook romantic dinners
using the moonlight concept and works of bereted surrealists.
The phone that's ringing is me wanting to know:
Is that a blue flower in your ear or have I been staring too long?
I can't remember any of my dreams, but I can
recall every detail of yours—including the one in the sidecar
and the scuba gear you donned so fetchingly that I turned
into a tropical fish and navigated between your breasts.
Because of you I plow into wooly snow banks daily,
I laugh at the money in my wallet, I speak
tongues as long as one of them is in your mouth.
I'm singing during my checkup, I'm swinging on—

yikes—your lianas in the rain forest, I'm committing to memory
the transcript of every single one of your previous tears.
I'm planning on crashing any weddings that get in my way
in hopes one will be ours. And because I can't figure out
what else to do with these wings, I'm always almost
ready to take flight off my roof into your arms.
One day I may turn into a cantor and I did not know
I owned a yarmulke. My unread books expose themselves
like exotic dancers, but modest ones, tricky with a feather boa.
Why, only last night a crank caller woke me at midnight
to tell me the true plot of *Twelfth Night*, for which I am
most glad. I am yodeling in subways. I'm moving so fast
I may as well be standing still. See? I'm the one
turning the corner right now, tugging on
the newfound string of the universe that's you.
Later if you need me I'll be working on that poem
in which I demonstrate your influence upon my life.

## Poem in which he explains exactly what it is he is working on:

Funding has come through at last, and that's why
everybody here will be busy on the Indolence Project
—just as soon as we wrap up the Oral History of
Disappointment. I think you of all people will appreciate
the difficulties we endured with Principles of Thigmotaxis
Among Declined Love-Interests. That's why we postponed
The Sex Life of the Thin-Skinned. There's a downside
to hitting it big when you're young, but was it my fault
I isolated the charisma-chromosome-deficiency
syndrome? That was still the seventies, but my Institute
was soon up and running: Cross-gender Winking Research...
Fun with Irony... Why This Dog Won't Hunt...
It would be great to feel the support of colleagues
like you once more, or at least if you would please
stop making a racket running the court upstairs.
If someone with your vision would consider taking
a seat on the Board we would find the collective will
to pursue Post-(P)sumo Wrestling, Tequila and I Forget,
Gnome on the Range & other Punnic Victories,
Strategies of Linguistic Enforcement: High School
Handbooks and the Rates of Recidivism in
*Catcher in the Rye*. We would stay on task,
be on point, break up into small groups and confer,
put our noses to the grindstone, our bodies to whipped
cream. (Where *did* you put the red shantung teddy?)
All day, the molecules chant like tonsured monks

and I knock down doors for words hiding inside.
Lately, the words have been *carapace*,
*louche*, and *rupestral*, but I'd like to report
progress on my new proposal for *ravishment*.

## Poem in which he goes to the exhibit, where he is ambushed:

If I never see another portrait
of the mild Virgin, one more tumescent nymph,
or a triptych of death and the sacred cross.
If I never see you in your midnight bath.
If I never see a ship ablaze,
if I never see rollicking peasants,
their elliptical loaves or their unworkable wooden shoes,
or wise guy gargoyles or slouchy burghers in floppy hats.
Let me see you with a sketch pad
in, let's say, autumn. If I never see the screech of
lines, tweaked cornfields, or a bandaged ear,
a girl reading or petting a little white dog,
if I never see the mismatched landscape
on either side of her misaligned face.
Spare me the stag that is tragically slain,
the dismounting king, the strife in the sunset,
spare me the sight of you on that landing.
Spare me dark woods in the midafternoon,
shadows cool as blades on the back of my neck,
the bird's cry yanking open my eyes,
the rustling in the brake and the crackling of twigs.
Spare me a summer you never returned.
See if I don't notice the delicate interplay of
light and dark, see if I don't stand in line to admire
the emperor's sarcophagus, see if I don't return
the look you give me touring the Vermeers.

## Poem in which he is a lion, including some wasted hours in Paris:

Once I was a hedgehog but now I like
being a lion. Most of your aardvaarks
caught on videotape will stipulate as much.
I have been known to be an ocelot,
but I think it's pretty obvious I am a lion.
Like all teenagers, I went through the phases:
possum, stingray, vampire, bison, regret.
I mean egret. Because I am now a lion
I don't worry about strangers circling my nest
anymore and can't be bothered to crawl in
my shell for the hike down to the eggy shore.
Of course, when I was a marlin I dreamed
I was a stallion and when I was a stallion
I dreamed I was singing like a meadowlark.
Once I swooped like a bluejay chockachawing!
and sampled like a giraffe the topmost leaves.
It was too much responsibility to timberwolf
around, to eagle upon the craggy heights.
Now time is a wormwood blur and I speak
impeccable French, a perfect lion. Maurice and Charles
present me the special menu, they light my unfiltered
cigarettes, they decant my wine through candlelight.
As I say, I am a lion. Sometimes I miss polar bear
when I wait in the parched clearing, for being
a lion is not all complex protein and carnivore games.
Everyone wants a piece, and when you walk in

the gallery you don't know what to look for,
or even how to look yourself, you are a lion.
When you write letters home, you start,
"Dear X, I'm sick to death in love with you
& I'm in Paris and X is not your name &
I'm sizing up a post-Cubist portrait by somebody
you have probably also slept with baroquely…"
The rooftops of Paris gleam with golden darts
—I think it must have rained since I was last out.
Then at the artist's reception I talk with somebody
who has skidding tire tracks for eyes. There are
bodies in the cellars, I admit to a sense of relief
you are in LA, that I don't have my own cri de coeur
or compensation package, I don't tell her
Sidney is my first name as well as my last. Success
I attribute to the excellence of my personal contacts
gleaned during those formative undergraduate years,
long before I was a lion. Do you like being watched
bathing in the river among other gazelles?
"Do you think a lion like me has a chance?"
"For what," she says, and tilts her champagne flute.
"And besides, remarks are not literature, but Sweet Jesus
you could try." Tomorrow I could end up an elephant,
I swear. My ears would fan the veld, my trunk
would swing like a philosopher armed with tenor sax.
Till then, I am a lion and I yawn in the teeth of the sun.

## Poem in which he is sick with love:

> *If you find my beloved, say I am faint with love.*
> *Say I am sick with love.*
> —Song of Solomon 5:8

Then say, right after, I'm sorry
about the former goldfish, the posthumous automobile,
the previous wisteria trimmed during the cherry cough
syrup sundae scenario. Say, before she steps on the gas,
I'll never preach to her again from a farther room.
Then say, she *did* look like a million bucks
in her new color, her new dress, her new do,
her new certification from the Institute. If you find
my beloved, ask her, does she need me to pick up
the dry cleaning, the shoe repair, or how about
the spring rolls and wonton soup she phoned in?
Convince her, I've had a good month or two
at work—without any sort of serious incident.
Tell her. Tell her *three*. Ask her how things go
with the new therapist—and tell her I regret
I did not make the appointment that time.
Is her trainer still Lance? Lance LaFlame? He seems
committed to her overall personal self-realization.
Tell her Snowy is checking for messages twice a day,
and that I don't seem to be allergic to Snowy as
I used to be. Tell her, I've waxed her pus-yellow Saab,
tuned it, and mounted four new replacement tires.
She'll know what I mean. *If you find my beloved,*

tell her I have established relations with my inner
Cro-Magnon, my outer orangutan, my median math score...
Look, just tell her, all right.
Is she seeing somebody else these days? What's his name?
Are the turkey leftovers still good to eat? And is she
aware of how much she owns fast approaches
the date of expiration? You can tell her, if you like,
I am finally picking up the subjunctive mood,
and finding everyday use for handy conditions which
are contrary, really fucking contrary to fucking fact.
Let her think I have reversed positions on
punishment capital, hockey ice, mother her.
Speaking of wine, tell her I have cellared a dozen
cases of the nineties, which I would love to sample
in the cool solemn darkness underground
with a tasty chèvre, like her, anyday.
Ask her if she's taking what I gave her for the pain,
something for that pinched nerve in her arm?
Find out if she saw the new moon last night over
the laminations of the bay out by San Quentin.
Remind her, I have sold the Vette, the blues tapes,
the gun, the boombox, and the leather bomber.
Say I was wrong about rap and about Bill Clinton,
wrong about the way the sun bounces off her eyes
that time on Mount Tam and everything I screamed
before lunch on the bike path when she slipped
and a cut bisected the perfect circle of her left
cheek. Tell her I've left all the album pages
blank, in case she brings the black and whites home.
Only, find my beloved. You know I am sick in love.
Plead for her number, beg if you have to for
the first letter of her name. Is that a G, like in Gretchen?
                    It is *Gretchen*?
I knew no way it was going to be Imogene.

127

## Poem in which he delivers the keynote address to the daily convention of those he let down:

Innocent bystanders and bisected guests. Flouncy and admonished
former flames. Once-upon-a-time not-insignificant others. Other
others. Professors and piano instructors. Coaches. Students
still hoping for letters of recommendation or final grades.
A special welcome to parents and family, especially
deceased. Please keep your admission stubs. First prize
in the drawing: solo dining at the half-star Obloquy Cafe.
Word is they work wonders with a suckling pig.
Something tells me lay off the lamb shanks, though.

So thank you for taking time out from your busy schedule
haunting my dreams. Can you hear up there in the cheap seats?
Good. This thing is on? Heartfelt thanks go out to participants
in this morning's panel sessions: "Snap Out of It."
"What Do You Mean, You Forgot?" "Seemed to Be
the Thing to Do at the Time." Would my offspring
please stand and take a bow? Just a thought, never mind.

I'd like to announce that I have finally unearthed
those missing opera tickets, and the aeolian harp,
and the metaphor for the old apple tree outside my window
that figures so prominently in several key unfinished works.
I'd like to add, too, that I now can lift my bat off
my shoulder and swing at that dubiously called strike three.
The search party I sent out is making solid progress on

the wedding album, the urns of dust and charred bone,
the satchel of love letters never quite sent soon enough.

In the little time I have left, I'd like to thank my friends
for sending me your books. I have figured out the software.
To my enemies who sent me your books, if you camp out
at the mailbox waiting, pack a hearty lunch. As for the Buick
Skylark, Percy, did you get the bouquet? I had no idea about
the tires. How could I know the soothsayer would not take
a personal check? Rupert, my best dog, I did all I could
for you in the end, and it was not enough to keep
your eyes from going flat as a camera lens. The plaid suitcase,
Marv, I did not know that's where you kept your best ideas
or that the new girlfriend would not find palatable my
hot tub reference. Hazaiah, I missed that moment
they broke into song and you strolled up to Jesus
and the sporting sun leaped like a marlin onto the hospital floor.

Finally, though, I've been sensing a little groundswell building
on behalf of the redevelopment project named Forgive Myself.
In that spirit, please reach under your chairs, go ahead.
Don those party hats and slip on your dancing shoes.
Any second Veuve Cliquot will come to a nearby glass.
Death, you see, is the lurking one in black tie and cummerbund,
dressed for the ball that coincides with the end of this event
called my life. He's not as tough as he seems, or was, or maybe is.
And trust me, there's nothing he can try anymore
that the expiatory rain hasn't already absolved.

# Poem in which he often is drowning:

Often as he feels himself dying in early June,
in New Jersey, he has just turned ten in God's pure love,
and when he drowns he goes into a smoked green glass

bottle. He pushes against the heavy sides and feels
the closing in, and the utter impossibility of clouds
in a presumable sky that carried Jesus, then Mary,

his mother, for a while away. Still, it's beautiful
almost down here. The trailing bubbles of expended air
remind him of the circles on the standardized answer sheet

for a vocational aptitude test that he filled in neatly
with his Number Two sharpened lead pencil, which
he did not forget to bring to school. Come to think of it,

there wasn't one single thing he ever forgot to bring
to school. Still, drowning is not much of a career move.
Or is it? Certainly, nothing like second Catholic President

of the United States. Nothing like Father Paul, Duke Snider,
Jimmy the Weasel, all the celebrities he ever knew.
But now he breaks out of the airtight bottle and

tumbles around like the stars, like science project molecules,
and the water is cold and heavy as mercury, and hitting bottom,
he kneads a few last desperate sculptures made of clay.

Below the surface, in the darkening deep, is where
he was always meant to be. These are the currents
he has always waited for, and his head fills up

with water and a true prayer. So he grows calm,
and begs God not to save him. To let him come
back to where he has always belonged.

Everything goes soft and black, like a hood
drawn down on his head, the equivalent of grace, of sleep,
the gentleness of things unknown, sweetness always to be

unperceived, moments never to savor or endure.
And it is perfect, drowning in this particular summer lake.
All the snapshots fade to black in their frames.

All the big decisions unravel, mistakes unmade.
All the lost hours reclaimed, lost lovers redeemed.
Give up the future for the prospect of eternity.

But it crosses his mind: perhaps these are Satan's real works
and his emptiest promises—to imagine a world without him,
a blank book, a bare canvas, an erasure, an eclipse.

—How it might have all been different, if someone else
had taken his place...forgotten the names of the people...
driven to the wrong destination...somehow said the wrong words—

Yet every time he is drowning in a particular summer lake,
a man is pulling him back up to the stifling air,
throwing his body with the certainty of heaven

onto the mud of shore. Just like that, thirty years
go by, shadows of flight on a summer lake, undoing of time,
and still he wonders how surviving could be
what it possibly means to be blessed.

**II**

## Poem in which he recalls those precious journeys with Wanda:

Wanda, we traveled from Pigs-in-Sunny-Abattoir, Hungary,
to Tourist-Train-Ambushed-Magic-Midnight, Mozambique,
from Fighter-Pilot-Dying-at-Dawn, Afghanistan,
to Bird-of-Paradise-Gash-Gold-Vermilion, Ring of Fire.
Such a tiny, combustible, fractious planet, don't you think?
We bought a thousand postcards and took snaps of the syllogisms.

My cherished Wanda, I still can't get through my head
how you managed to speak, wherever we went,
in the local patois. Was it in Pakistan or Peru you ventured,
in perfect idiom, "My feet take two steps before I do,"
and they rose and cheered and picked up our check?
Where is there now left for me, dearest Wanda, to go?

True, once, a very lonely night, we fell in love, though
I attribute that one indiscretion to the influence
of the sun's pouring through the stained glass epic tale
of martyrs, wise men, and the babe in swaddling clothes.
We share a weakness for reliquaries and acedia.
And the cathedral crushed us, that and the grappa flask.

I still see you on every empty platform, in shadows
of flight, in the fast-changing weathers. I still seek you out
in the back of planes, in cafes, on all the crowded streets.
Recall when once we came upon a weeping schoolgirl
near a fountain in Rome? We took to the hotel for a week.

Now, the leopards enfilade the gusting savannah
and my lungs are ventilated by your blood.

## Poem in which he looks to find his voice:

I decompensated the galleria shopkeeper,
ladling out 17 billion lire, one by one,
a bargain for a first-edition blazing bonfire.
But in the split second while I admired those
perfect teeth of hers and tried to put the past
behind me and the busted transmission and cracked
daguerreotypes I was momentarily entranced
by those mordacious green eyes, slightly carnal,
and just like that when I turned back to where
I thought my voice was handy, it was gone.

I searched but it did not lurk among fluorocarbons,
wasn't lounging inside the socks drawer, wasn't
growling with the other joists after the temblor.
I sought it out amidst the yowls at the pound,
the speckled one with cocked ear had me going.
It wasn't in the jar of cold coins, it wasn't stuck
on the windshield, it wasn't tap dancing in the shoe
mausoleum. I cracked the spines of my seven books,
soaked off the wine labels, combed the factotum's
hair. Underneath the eggs in the nest abandoned,
stripping off dry wall tape, snapping with laundry
on a windy clothesline, south of central miasma,
north of the hierophants. Tub filling with beer,
the rustling alarum of a rabbi's beard, plaid skirt

of a school girl, tugging on a turkey wishbone,
hoping world peace, engine turned over, dust on a road,
guitar pick and sickle, swoop of a raven wing,
refrigerator hum, snap of finger, slap of face,
butane shush, wheelchair hum, rose petal scoop
over corporal nakedness, which was my default dream setting,
and much more compact than my gamma ray burster.


My vermilion flyers fluttered on martial telephone poles.
For a long time after I'd slow down at the corners,
parts of town where other voices go to get right.
I resolved if ever I got my voice back
I would not lend it out or let it run loose again.
Once I heard someone telling a few whoppers
at a Beverly Hills party and I thought for a second:
that could be my voice. I recognized the twang,
the tinny majorettes at the grand parade. Thus I was
unsurprised when the kidnappers' note appeared.
They wanted a ransom of two rainbows and the environs
of Seattle. A small price to pay, I knew,
so I threw in the Green Bay Packers and my rewrite
of *Wuthering Heights*, a less comic update, if you will.
It was worth it, every penny, every radiance, each
raindrop and mocha latte, when I saw my voice
step off the biplane and trip across the tarmac
toward my feathery arms. So much to catch up on,
ground to cover, tattoos to send out for bleaching.
Tell me what's with the accent, which I still can't place.

## Poem in which we hear the latest news from the far West:

For love he would squeeze her a thousand oranges
if she wanted them, would lurk through the dark hours
outside and scavenge in the hen house for the fresh
green and speckled eggs at dawn.
He would pound out the loaves of bread
at the bakery or deliver the milk or the morning
paper in the big white truck. If she wished.
Or he would make her coffee black and strong
the way he liked it, or let her tea steep and then
slightly cool. He'd knock down a tree for
the honey and ladle it into her wordless mouth.
If he was just crazy, why would he return,
what use would he have for a gun,
for the ax, for the maps of the trails, for
the magazines they'd soon put her prom picture in?

## Poem in which while judging a spelling bee he has a minor breakdown over "argillaceous":

Contestants palpitate on the grade-school
stage, and their dental appliances shimmer
like quaking aspen in the coltish breeze.
Roots and stems bulge in their pockets,
backpacks jammed with Greek, Latin, Sanskrit,
and cheese. Silent P acts like a psychopath,
silent B, a lot like a lamb on a limb.

A sybil tells sibilant anecdotes in the pharmacy, too,
and diachronic ecdysiast is a shibboleth to them,
who gallivant with any lepidopterist
while ichthyologists converge.
The contestants are not dyspeptic,
though one stumbles on the sentinel's armamentarium
and another chokes down a cicerone with a macaronic.
No, this oeuvre is batrachian as a swamp,
and no chatelaine is safe, no satrap, podesta, or paladin.
Put on your plenipotentiary's swaddling clothes
reeking of frankincense, parsimony, and myrrh!

"Can you use that word in a sentence please?"
He locates the notecard and reads into the mike.
*Giddy with quotidian antibiotics,*
*he lopes across the argillaceous ground.*
Which of course is way too pellucid to live.

The judge wonders why it is he can't spell.
He pulls out the CAT scan and discreetly examines
his cerebral cortex. There on the brain map where
words go to be spelled a For Sale sign towers in
a vacant lot advertising COMMITMENT, while
a rat which lives in SEPARATE forages in grey dark.

So rises he unshod and interprets *argillaceous*
as if he's Martha Graham, and graphs it on a handy x/y axis,
and stretches his canvas, swabbing it twelve colors of mood.
He'd been invited to rip off the words' bandages
but he didn't think he'd irrigate the origin of wounds.

## Poem in which he devours the white wolf:

I noticed the climate in the fairy tales
had suffered a change, and musty discolorations

of pages turned amber, and slowly
the sky filled with illegible migrations,

which are the accounts of childhood. So when the day
turned porcelain, stainless steel, and white tile,

windowless fluorescence and high ceilings, my eyes
smarting from the glint on the tables that were

loaded down with a hundred surgical knives of
divers lengths and purposes, I felt in a manner of speaking

prepared. That moment, it all changed, into trivial sunlight,
and small romantic tables, postcard hotels and bistros,

bottles of wine translating the brightness,
an enormous prism in the doorway catching it all,

letting the purple, the gold, the red and blue sadness
stain the walls. And then day just kept turning

over and over, fast, from book to hospital to hotel,
from harbor, to vineyard, to cemetery,

from roads home to roads out of town,
from robbery of the grave, to Mass, to lovemaking,

all the way to the high flat country I never knew
and the cellars of my house swimming with storied rats,

teachers with apples and federal agents,
husbands and their wives, anthropologists,

ones thinking music, doing the calculus, ones
discussing string theory for hours over canapés.

That's only a fire examining my house.
You know from the drills how you're supposed

to touch a door first before you open.
If it's hot, you should stay put.

What if the door is always hot?

## Poem in which appear the special children:

Tonight, if not everywhere, special children restless
are, are in their cribs, parents arriving unto them
while buoyant their heads arrhythmical kiss
the slick red spongy big bars of the bed.

So, and so, special children turn quiet
in their littler rooms, start to otherwise
laughing on dirty jokes the shoes are telling,
the shattering stars, the shit in their golden pants.

Sometimes, you know, getting angry are these,
the special children, with swooping down phones,
and coffee cups that must spill up, sometimes
new pictures need to be cracked open on the walls.

Special children are being thought of
running, and all go falling down in lonely malls.
From the corners of the mouths they're only bleeding.
Their slow eyes slide when they cry to the sleeping.

Can they be now sleeping? Just, please be sleeping?

## Poem in which he catalogues instances of touch:

The nimbus of a basketball's nub.
Two of your most precious toes.
The snout of a stand-up comic crocodile.
But breasts, now, they lead the pack.
The soft pointy ear of a mouse, misfortunately.
The coat of a white whippet named Edwina.
A caftan embroidered with a thousand tea roses.
A stack of Ben Franklins on a felt table.
The bronze handle of the casket.
The score for *West Side Story* dancing
off the piano in the wind storm.
But let's not lose contact with breasts.
Your hair, falling on my face, next pillow.
That pillow, recovered after being lost
all night and on its own, but now held close
and cool to my chest, which made me
sleep through the alarm and the interview
with Allied Mythmakers, "full-service agent
to the stars." The stars. I didn't know they could
be touched but now they flutter in my grasp
like the wings of a moth I can't quite coax
away from the lamp, even when I carry it
tickling my palms to the door and
I have to turn off the lamp and sit
in darkness gone ridged as corduroy.
The darkness: sometimes the brush

of an echolocating misunderstood mammal
crucial to the ecology of the world where we live.
Sometimes a 2 x 4 or the plumage of a macaw.

**Poem in which he, despite being historically the sort of student who falls in love with his teachers, struggles with foreign language acquisition:**

So you can't roll your R's, can't trill your L's,
and you can't cluck a Q to save your life.
Still, Study In Your Spare Time CDs
constantly chirr in your pachydermatous ear.
But when you ask the concierge for a room with bath
all you manage to express is a wish to attend
the Piltdown Man Show at high noon.
So much you intend is lost in translation's blitz.
I refer to the time the florist went blank
when you remarked on her crazy escutcheon.
And what did you expect the gendarme to do
when you told him that you required
the services of a radiant neurosurgeon?
And then at the superrealist's benefit bash
you apologized for losing your head in a fuggish canoe.

Run your tongue on the braille of the other's world.
Brush up on verbs of betrayal and ennui.
Forget nouns, carry pronouns in a sack
tied with a string of exclamation points.
Pick a fight, if you must, with a *slow* ontologist.
Do not pass up any opportunity to
disarm a bomb in a revolutionist's gym bag.
Before long you will be conversing with whales,
the parrot will come around to your point of view,

and you will lope alongside the family dog
tracking the silent whistle's commensal source.
Learn the right gifts to break a heart,
when to order one more shot than you can use,
how to get a beauty's attention on the strand
while you're surfing the riptide.
How to dress the lines for the blizzard that's due,
how to ululate till a clerk's brain seizes
and you can steal the sunglasses of your dreams.
One day, your regrets will sleep upside down
like bats in the vowels. For now, let's familiarly address
the sun and let's inscribe red X's on names you use for love.
If you want to take her breath away though
just make your lips do this.

## Poem in which he looks past the problems of relationship and forges ahead dreamily:

I said it was like falling asleep nowhere
and waking in some beautiful new country
and if I can get a visa I want to inhabit you
like the beautiful country you are
on the long continent of the late afternoon
in the middle of the season of nothing else is
where the phone never rings again or just once more
a reminder of everything else taking place everywhere else

I will distribute the glossy blue postcards
and tack this poster up on the wall
with diamond studs from your ears
Here are the local instructions about local customs
local water local food and festivals
so you will know precisely
what I do not mean

There may be birds but nothing as indifferent
as condors or eagles or swans
and all you know and I will know
(I can't keep you out of this)
is how the trees keep shedding music
at, say, four o'clock. *Say, Four o'clock…*
by which I mean to say right now

brushing aside the possibility of insurrection
the political independence of this tropical paradise
the question of the rainy season coming on
and the problem of the rainy season coming on

## Poem in which "To think at this late date...":

...we bolt upright from bed in a cold sweat
fearful we, have misplaced a comma.

Later we check to see our socks match
and if it's time to resuscitate the couplets.

To think, we consume fossil fuel to rush across
town to catch the dinosaur symposium.

At this late date, so much at this late date.
We charm, we please, we scrape, we mewl, we carp

around buffets, backstage, the cruise, I am
bic pentameter, to think this is called for anymore.

That we sleep on sheets, that we still cook the meat,
that we're impressed by the rouged dossier of

her cheeks, to think at this late date we compose
our most challenging work thus far.

That this is the path to the waterfall, that the sound
the sky makes is the applause of a thousand wings,

that the clearing is anything but and the white
light in the harbor still guides us along

at this late date, to think I almost never knew you,
that we stroll vanquished into the squawk and squeal,

the hum and whoosh of the woods, to think at this late date
we want to know how we and the poems will end.

III

## Poem in which he attempts an answer to Pablo Neruda's question—"In the end won't death be an endless kitchen?":

Hey, that's my *mother's* endless kitchen!
The fierce whiteness of eggs,
the bread that sighs in our hands.
So much cinnamon dust we can't stop
laughing, my brother and I.  Baskets
of apples, red bell peppers, tomatoes,
mounds of brown sugar and saharas of salt,
parma hanging like an ampersand on a hook.
Garlands of rosemary, parsley, and basil.

(Speaking of Neruda, I once walked around
his Isla Negra home, and he owned lots of things
for a Marxist, including dolls, hats, guns, masks,
and one papier-mâché stallion. He also set up
his bar on a boat docked in a flagstone courtyard
elevated a hundred yards from shore.)

To return to death, I would argue with Neruda
about nothing, but in my mother's endless kitchen,
she is always storming: "Who let the jaguar in again!"

The sun is blocked by a cloud of confections
and sapiential grapes stock the bookshelves.
I've never once used the word "tranquil"
without paying for it, so I won't point up
how the sea shakes and leaps like fire

when we blow the candles out, when we let
the meandering stars stream inside.

Tonight, Neruda, my mother's singing
her one aria, she who could never carry a tune.
We have a notable absence of fens in here
and dragons foraging among the bones.
Tonight, even I can write the saddest lines
while she is liminally framed, ascending her stairs,
going up always where endlessness begins.
So we'll wash our dishes till sunup
and listen for the music from her forest of spoons.

## Poem in which he is driving westward and it's Good Friday:

Need a God by whom electroconvulsive
therapy would be contraindicated of me.
Need a God to walk with me alongside
The Seratonin Reputake Blockered
Happy People, need a God, I think.
Need a God, to struggle with me,
cast me down, snap a good rib of me,
need, OK *need*, a God.
Need a God to raze the whole house of me,
torch fields, books, flood the cellars of me,
as I think I've implied, need a God.
Need a plan, need some sleep, need a God,
need rain, need sun, need idea, need a God.
Need a God to help me select with
my non-exist slash high-paid decorator "Margot"
chic blackout blinds for me,
contemplate otherwise balanced breakfast for me.
Need a God to go over with me
news re: friends, loss of. Need a God
to help keep track, need a God
to wake me with slap, need a God
to lift me, not drop me down to tiled,
mosaic floor. Help me in muck,
in mire, the bog, on mountain making
those shadows over me, or bottom of the lake,
in friendly convenient all-night liquor

stores, a God's name on my lips, a God
whose name is always on my lips. God, need
new voice, new words, God, to get this rock
off the chest of me, God,
take ice cube out of the mouth of me.
Take the wheel, go on, you can.
And play music you like, go ahead.
Just play. We'll make this our little ritual.
Our uniforms come ripped from the stars.
And right here, at the curve, I'll stop
so you can see Asia if you want.
See the sea shining black like flanks of a horse?
Later, all right? I wish you'd please drive.
Seems like it's not my car.

Your test results are back. I'm taking a look at your book.

## Poem in which he is harangued by the minor Old Testament prophet Habakkuk, about whom, conveniently, nothing is known:

Just don't count on this being the night you pen
"One could do worse than be a swinger of birches."
And that's not neuralgia coming on—it's me
banging the pizza-sized tambourine in your ear.
You think I'm impressed you're sleeping with
half the girls calling themselves Colette in New York?
I don't care that you're big and heartless in the city,
that you juggle three pugs, that you have a plot
of fictional purple tulips, that you know how
to work the vodka, the moon, and a straight razor.

My wrath is like a river. My God, why do the righteous
suffer? Why do the evil laugh at every fortress?
I'm going to stand at my runic watchpost
and raise my tablets when you run by in your darkness.
For I may be a minor prophet but I do know you:
The time you flung your sandals from the rope bridge
into the gorge, and the Thai girl Meow in Phuket
where kickboxers' sweat landed in your Singha.
She seemed to read what was left of your mind,
later washed her platinum hair in your sink.
This is the night I put everything else in. This is flying
home. This is song. This, the house in flames.
This is the night you lick the girl's soles till she screams.
You have not been yourself since the crows

decided on your garden, since that, you know, war.
Your test results are back. Am taking a look at your book.

## Poem in which he explains how you may best prepare for reading *The Brothers Karamazov*:

I would practice your spitting and sputtering from
stupendous heights. I would cultivate a healthy respect
for testamentary salvoes ventured from the ice floes.
I would not personally tango with a bear I was not
already acquainted with. I would contemplate rumors
spread by a quorum of dysfunctional lynxes.
I would pray—and to God, too. I'd lift outsized
Chinese chests if they were painted orange or red,
consume the contents of the nearest carp pond.
I'd reorganize the address book and resolve never
to lose another phone number. I would find an excuse
to stick around for the conclusion of a conversation
that begins *The night is a shield I have plundered!*
But I belabor the obvious, all of you kneeling in stained
cassocks are too polite to point up. Nobody is
polite in *The Brothers K,* which fact is refreshing as gelid
frozen vodka before you meet your one o'clock World Lit
class at one-twenty-five. I would not celebrate the rosy
cheeks of any nubile creature unless I meant
business. I would always mean business even if I had
no business to mean. I would save my stray kopecks,
I would introduce myself to the Orthodox Icons,
I would not trim my beard on the Sabbath, I would
not kidnap the progeny of any Czar or Czarina.
I'd learn, if I had to, Russian. I would submit early
my request to be reborn in Petersburg. Then let's you

and me challenge the first rake of a cavalry captain
we come across to a duel. He's smacked our fathers
with the heel of his glove, he's plowed our fields under,
he's seduced our sisters and stolen the family diadem.
Later we break into houses and drown the parched plants.

**Poem in which there is the ultomato, as well as his
grandfather, and comes close to quoting Gertrude Stein,**
*Picasso: "When he ate a tomato the tomato was not
everybody's tomato"*:

My grandfather grew those tomatoes.
Pasquale grew tons of tomatoes
and tied my father to a post in the cellar
when he was bad and beat him
in the dark. The world. It is starving
and his children are stuffed with his tomatoes.

When my grandfather ate a tomato
his tomato was not anyone else's tomato.

*In the rows of vegetables, zucchini,
broccoli, and corn, painted on my canvas,
rows of eggplant, basil, and tomato,
I find rabbit pellets and silvery tracks of
snails assuming cubist formations.*

I recall Pasquale in the kitchen,
eating a tomato while the whole house reeks
of vinegar, olive oil, and red peppers,
while the chicken spatters in the hot pan,
and I can still see—

my grandfather bowing his head on Sunday
at Our Lady of Perpetual Pomodoro Church

as Father Rosario raises his hands to heaven,
his vestments embroidered with vines.

## Poem in which he considers indifference at midnight (after a line by Philippe Soupault, "*Comme l'indifférence est belle à minuit*"):

Indifferent at seven-forty-five, or dawn, that I get.
But used to be, come midnight you would catch me
going, "That's a fascinating brooch you've broached,
tell me more about your animadversions!" Or, "Sure,
we've got plenty of gas to get to the summit," or,
"Hey, let's do that one again, but first how about
a bite of your little madeleine?" Cute, perhaps fetching,
possibly oleaginous, but beautiful? I would have
kept that one in reserve. No more though.
Beauty, rubicund wonder, be my midnight now.
Lethargy is passé, remoteness, de rigueur.
Dénouement, éminence grise, fait accompli,
ménage à tuna—there, I've used up most of
French One. Oh, and décolletage, a favorite.
Midnight was the time to start your paper on
"*Heart of Darkness*: Cardiac Arrest?"
That's when you banged out the Bangor File,
when you hammered out terms for
the Hammerman Account. You catch a game,
you order onions on the burger and care less,
you tell the guy on the Harley to move his piece
of crap. Later, you walk the floors midnight
with your child in your arms, waiting for
ampicillin to kick in, hoping your own crepitant
melodies could salt him into sleep.

My Beautiful Midnight Indifference.
Well, it is a relief from midnight desiring,
rambling, scowering, seizing, sneezing.
Those are lovely handles it has, that's velvet
lining the cedar box, we've got hours till
morning and nobody I can see's laughing.
I think I'll always miss, though, the frisson
of a shooting star and the busted tail light
entrée to those who would serve and protect
our community from people like me.
So what if I can't promise always to be
indifferent at midnight? I'm committed still
to my rowdy nap in the trope of the afternoon.

## Poem in which he directs a pretentious, critically acclaimed low-budget movie and it's obvious he's never even been to film school:

*Golden carriages arrive*         *pulled by black horses*

We have lived our lives in this hard steady rain
one day it seems to abate      but this calm
becomes an aspect of the storm      this silence
is luminous a moment      Inside of me the horses breathe
The trees take root in the lungs
The curtains exhale      and just by holding to
this ledge      just by looking out there
And under the colonnade      in my white suit
the stairway crawls down to you      I desiderate
into a language I cannot control      more inflected
my God than Greek      My words become steps and
on the edge of my tongue you trip and fall
into the opening ground     we speak     in another tongue
In the movie      you and I lose what remains of our lives

*Yellow carriages arrive*         *pulled by red horses*

Of course we have the man with a blue patch over
his left eye      Unceremoniously he shoots the chandelier
The tapestry is set aflame      The anchorite wanders off
into the wood      the carved railings take him in
chandelier falling      the complex music      splintering
absolute tonality      Nature is defeated      No cry

of a pathetic songbird needs to be compared
and the translucent voice          the spectral song
This man with a blue eyepatch takes dead aim at
the sky and misses everything          draws a bead on
the ground and fires into the heart of the sun
Until the next frame          Yes, the perfect crime

*Green carriages arrive          pulled by blue horses*

My gradual eyes focus on the distance which is
an oak tree          and the red clouds frame it against
the hills          Cut away          Pick up the birds of prey
circling          Cut to the clouds swelling on the horizon
Now cut to the white wolves silent in the arms
of the tree          They have come for me I know
I am miserably equipped with my disguises
as I walk through my part as the rain on the lake
as the drowning in the lake          as the boat loosely moored
as the glass shattering on the floor          as the fire
kindled in the grate          everywhere as cloud chandelier curtain
Cut back to
*white carriages drawn by white wolves*
*white wolves driving white carriages*

## Poem in which illustrious Occam shaves:

That spare, angular Occam.
He stropped his razor sharp and clean
and eliminated

uncertain speculations about
reality. He'd spent his working day
trimming overgrown

hedges wherever he found them.
So he left his razor in
the toilet streaked

with stale lather and black stubble.
This bitter, lonely Occam.
So I took up that same razor.

And then it was no longer April
with rose petals drifting in
the breeze, no soft raining,

it was just you sitting across
the room. I was not still
as water looking on you,

only nervous, your voice would not
pass for mandolin, your eyes jade,
your hair the long wheat fields.

That failed man. You were your interpretation.
I put his razor back,
regard the mere clouds,
pursue the black dragons.

**Poem in which he considers plagiarizing a poem by Robert Desnos (1900–1945), you know, the one that, translated, begins, "There is a precise moment of time / When a man reaches the exact center of his life":**

I was screaming at my Muse, it was three a.m.,
she looked like shit, and what made her
think she was my Muse anyway, hanging out
biker bars, the MLA, pouring my troubles into
others' ears, giving away my ideas for poems
as if poems had ideas, some kind of Muse,
I used to count on her, I used to please her,
take her where she told me to go. Now, I can't
stand hearing about her former liaisons,
Mistress Bradstreet, Browning, George Herbert,
the list goes on. As if I care, I mean, why
can't she tell this is the middle of my life?
Doesn't she know the signs? I'm writing
sestinas. I'm organizing the postcards for
the lucky college archive yet to be named.
Must I remind her about the terminal disease?
Must I make a fool of myself yet again
in the gazebo at the lawn party? I am
detecting a pattern in her behavior.
I am detecting I'm not in it. Why does
she dress like everybody else, and whose idea
was the hair? That was me, at the park,
drinking wine, struggling with a rhyme
for "orange," which she gave me but which

I forgot. I'm in the middle of my life.
It's high time she proves she loves me
best of all. I'd forgive her, if she would.
Now, Muse, just tell me, what do I have
to say for myself? Don't leave me hanging
till next Friday, when the exact middle of my life
is scheduled to come back around.

## Poem in which Orpheus rearranges the world yet again:

All day long the mountains
kept falling down at his feet.
All day long he put them back up,
rearranging the clouds for Hollywood special effect,
far as the eye could see uprooting the solitary trees,
answering their informal requests, for no fee at all,
to stand in a pleasant grove.

When he appealed to his flute,
commensurate with his responsibility,
the avalanche was quickly arrested,
the hurricane subsided, having no better idea.

So why now, here in his room, the garden,
snacking on olives, does he recall
that woman he couldn't turn his back on,
and hum a tune, putting the whole world naturally
to sleep, not in his personal darkness but in its own continuing light?

Now nothing to look forward to—except for that dream
of being torn in every imaginable direction.
And the mail from his admirers stacked up in the corner
and tomorrow more benefits for the underground.

**Poem in which he depends upon a passing familiarity with the works of Sir Walter Scott:**

Marchetti could not hit the ball that far.
But then he did. I don't know. I do not know.
A pitch that hung out over the letters? a tipped off changeup?
a batting practice fastball across the fat white heart of the plate?
From right field I couldn't really be sure of anything—
except Marchetti had somehow hit a home run and we'd lost
another game.
Sir Walter Scott had a different idea.

We called the center fielder Sir Walter Scott.
He wore a shiny suit to the school dances,
he was the only one to get through *Ivanhoe*
with his eyes wide open at the end.
On the school bus to the games, where the pro scouts
wrote him up, he'd just stare out the window,
intent on something most of us couldn't contemplate.
"Willie Scott's bat and glove do the talking," said the papers.

So when Marchetti connected, Sir Walter Scott took off,
refusing to accept the obvious, turning his back to the plate,
throwing himself at last up against the top of the fence.
It sounded like a transmission
dropping to the street, like gears grinding.
And his body seemed to gather itself up in midair
before it fell down in slow double and triple folds,
like a dress did in our collective fantasies,

like hedge clippings on a hot Saturday afternoon,
like a movie pirate's doubloons glinting in the sun
while Marchetti kept circling the bases
as if it mattered, and the ball came to rest
in the mucid javelin pit. In a few years, a body bag
would remove Willie from another field.

Playing ball with my son today on the same field,
catching my breath on the warning track,
minty explosions of cut grass in the air,
the same eucalyptus trees shedding their bark
and straining like us to free themselves of the earth,
I turned for one last time, hoping now
Marchetti would be thrown out at the plate,
and found myself running and standing still all at once,
toward Walter Scott there on the grassy meads,
tilting forever in his shimmering mail, as if
baseball were played as it should be in the clouds.

IV

VI

## Poem in which he faces a firing squad after weeks of reading Latin American fiction:

When geese scatter and dogs
on porches wake with
a start and conversations in
the square come to a halt and
children suddenly abandon
their games and while bullets
hang suspended in midair
as leaves do when
they drop and seem to
be conflicted by wind
blindfolded from what
I failed to notice anyway in
the end unable to say the right thing
to those I wished to love
about the eclipsing beast's
countenance glued to the inside
of my reflection and on the leaf
I would inscribe the story of
my life while somewhere the leaf drifts
down in a wood I have never known
and the hummingbird shoots up
in dust lit gold as I pass this time
across unfallen leaves on a walk
that I plan on dreaming
does not ever stop.

## Poem in which the concept of *closure* is addressed:

Bitter pill, closure.
Astronaut food, a sandwich of wonder bread.
Cinders in the salad, bonfires of toothpicks.
When did the madman pick all the locks?
Where's your sherpa when you need one?
You know once you get the bumblebees talking
they are impossible to stop. They want us to taste
their hunger, to introduce us to the queen
but who needs a queen? Some places I never leave
are places I've never been. Take that turret
for instance, and a certain princess whose braids
tumble down for me to clamber to her rescue.
I am thinking of the ocean floor, making change
for a gold doubloon and the treasure of the casket
jammed with old photographs. When I stood
on the veld there was stampede of zebra,
which I also could not leave. There are docks
and there are doorways where I can still be found
going over the mail and the misery of passng time.
You know how the night inks your eyes clear
of light and you're the last one off the carousel?
You know when you spin a globe and stop it
with your thumb in the middle of Mozambique?
That's me, striding along, a wily baritone,
a snake jar on my head, but some places,
say alongside you, never come round again.

The last place I wrote you was the Sierra retreat.
As before the potbelly stove was overrun with ants.
At sunset the deer came down for a good drink.
The piano stood upright and tragic after the quake
that littered the field with bric-a-brac and closure.
Bees, be quiet for once. Sun, stay glued to my face.

## Poem in which he posits several inevitabilities:

He thought the Tragic Muse sneezed in his ear on
The Fourth of July, but it was just a brass oom-pah-pah
band oom-pah-pah in the Tuileries oom-pah-pah.
Whenever he's at a loss, he makes a fancy allusion.
Seems that Roger Maris, year after he hit sixty-one,
ate nothing but escargots. For real. Then McGwire
went for seventy. Only in gauze-gowned retrospect seems it
inevitable. When he spies a bovinian Constable,
surrender he must to a bucolic urge and take a good
walking stick and a crew of border collies back to
the mother ship. Oh, amours of loony selenographers.
It's not impossible, to have had another life.
The trick is to live free of epistemological presuppositions
and a totalitarian country with state-sponsored terrorism.
Now, when he hears the cockroaches' wings—
that's a bad omen for party guests who won't leave
and need the bathroom yet again and it puts a crimp
in his postprandial designs with the one whose voice
makes him feel itchy inside and under his scalp.
Damn roaches. They will inherit the earth, which
is 90 percent bacteria, though after final faculty evaluations
he would have guessed more. Some nights are long ones
that's for sure, when he can't quite sleep or stay
awake, and he eats a bowl of cereal in company with TV.
One time it was *Othello*, and there was no time to lose.
The general will wobble off again, and he will orate

his life away to the late-arriving impotentates.
Something's a little bit wrong with his imagination, too,
the way it sets him up for disappointment and not just
on summer vacation, but he can't change even a little
his wish to change just a little, not to mention the moue
of a Constable, a damsel, and a killer with a quick delivery.

## Poem in which he addresses some problems with fathers:

Besides mortality, let's not ignore the superventions du jour.
How many brain cells bite it on the way to morning
while you uncap a bottle and count off the stars?
I digress, but. What happened and what was made up
and what's the difference? Was there a puppy? Did you play
catch till the sun winked above the, I don't know, *oak tree*?
You're pretty sure you didn't go to *Turandot* or flip off
a manta ray at $H_2O$ *World*. The combination you devise
for letting somebody know you were in love. Trouble
with fathers is that the lake sloshes against the endless wharf,
and you can't get over how shark skin feels so much like
his chin stubble, and when you change the oil in the car
you watch him pass down the street into another life.
Trouble with fathers is the trouble with, could be, me.
A twig that snaps underneath my boots in darker woods.
Rifle report that stops mid-echo a caw from completion.
The trouble with fathers has to do with fingerprints
on the windowsill of your old room, where you climbed in
after a night of practicing how to switch gears,
play defense with your feet, keep your eyes open
when taking a punch, roast black a red pepper and put
it inside a paper bag to sweat, tie a Windsor knot,
negotiate a mortgage and a plot with a prime bay view,
take care of your mother, take care, care, care, care.

## Poem in which angels see what they see at twilight:

*"[Augustine] called 'morning knowledge' the angels' knowledge of things in their primordial being...and 'evening knowledge' their knowledge of created reality..."*
—Aquinas

At water's edge of wire-service photographs
snapped in the aftermath of twisters, quakes, floods,
and forest fires, count on seeing the dogs. Sometimes
they prance through devastation on leashes,
sometimes they stare out from newsprint, beg for bone
or tennis ball to be thrown. You see them dig through
rubble, seeking out anybody's besotted love.
The world is overrun with angels, but twilight ones,
since that's our sort of world. That's what makes a hawk
miss a lucky field mouse. Hand it to them, though,
they're busy, the twilight angels, cuing up
migrations of endangered birds and butterflies,
rearranging sand castles, losing receipts and reasons
to live, getting hung up inside the silo or the wine bin.
They're turning up the volume in the storm, telling you
it's closing time, whittling the telephone poles into
pencils, holding up the day's final ski lift for you to ascend.
They whisper, Gaze back into the stranger's eyes one
second more. They are good with your friend's money
and bad with sympathy cards, loose with praise
and tight with advice. They have little stake in keeping
your marriage or integrity intact, so that's why

they're doing checkout in the express line,
chalking up the victim on the sun-pliant asphalt.
They won't hurry you out of the salon once the brawl's
in full swing. And then when you make your grand
entrance with the headless horse, they erase the words
you memorized and grant redundant permission
to sing an unscripted ditty, dance a tarantella.
That's what they do best, the twilight angels,
they wander deserts because they know how
the movie has to end and won't tell you why.
And after high tide traps the scout troop inside the sea
cave, starfish intumesce on the xanthic shore.
The angels seed the rainy roads from a basket of ball bearings.
They take up residence in the vacated rooms,
they answer breathlessly the phone when you're out
and promise to write down the message if they find a pen.

## Poem in which he corrects at the press conference the erroneous news reports:

I caught, OK, this morning morning's minion,
surgically implanted the chirp and the microchip,
and unlatched the mnemonic cage. Also, that shoplifting charge
was dismissed when I proved those seraphic choir
robes were destined eventually to be mine. I am not in fact
an only child and I was technically never adopted once
in my life. Hirsute and bejeweled denizens of
The Fourth Estate, be informed it was I who fomented
riots in the hibernaculum over my self-imposed production quotas,
I who organized demonstrations of anthropomorphic animals
against myself and my spavinizing farm policies.
My taxes and milk cartons are what you'd call current,
I am bullish on the matador market, never sucked
on metal I did not find precious, and the inside-
trader info pertaining to self-ironing chinos con tequila
will not be traced back to me. Now, as for those compromising
photographs I posed for when I was an undergrad
cosmology student in need of rent money, I want
you to know the legumes were not my idea.
I did marry seven times, but all to the same woman,
and as the mopey liar and dyslexic Heraclitus once opined,
you cannot really step into the same residue twice—
not that any red-blooded American won't mostly try.
Beyond that, my spiritual inclinations are nobody's biz
but Jesus's, and I take no credit for discovering the internet,
foreshadowing, cambozola cheese, or the Pythagorean theorem.

So you want dirty linen? You like a skeleton in the closet?
All right. Once I found solace in a Cancun cabana,
but the cerveza was cold and the slippery sea had pulled
the murky curtain down on the estivating matinee,
if I may be so bold as to ask you to butt out.
I spilled a pint of my own blood on the files,
but only because I could not get her to budge.
Soon after I was the first astronaut in space blessed
with acrophobia, tenure, and a mild case of the mange,
but I have since resettled on terra firma,
two-thirds in love with easeful gravitas.
I did unmoor the heiress's balcony rails
though not for those reasons ruthfully alleged.
I'm stuck on an old desire to navigate a cloud,
to coruscate competitively with a chandelier,
I'm stuck, which I want to make perfectly clear.
I want to inoperate the formerly operative assertions.
Success will never go to my head. Murals are on mirrors,
my eyes shaded with trompe l'oeil tape, all of the above
opted for on the standardized examinations.
Finally, when spring roisters about who does not feel
anxious as a man on the brink of executive clemency?
That's when flying buttresses take wing. I've always
placed my faith in the kindness, you know, of swimmers,
how they let me flail and flop in the fast lane
of the lap pool. My favorite color is a shadow
beamed by a tocsin moon. As you asked me to do,
I have reviewed my notes and the video.
I never actually claimed I was going to live forever.

**Poem in which an escape takes place:**

Each day carries an alias, an airtight alibi,
a great scheme to get rich or free quick.
I drive the getaway car and my fingerprints
litter the paths of my escape like the ashes
of burnt banknotes and stolen securities,
the only kind in the world I could acquire.
So in the end, who would not squeeze the trigger,
sign someone else's flamboyant name, light
the bomb and run?
                                Crossing statelines, into Kansas,
watching the exodus of blackbirds from the snapping
wires, who would not look up and see, somewhere
in the distance, El Dorado, Elysium, Oz, California?

**Poem in which he has trouble with this elegy for Bathsheba's first husband, Uriah, a loyal soldier whose death in war was neatly arranged by King David, who would become her second:**

But hold on, not so fast,
let's not get started, otherwise
there would be the Absalom Absalom
stuff memorialized by Faulkner
—and a son's death due to a
father's folly is too much pain,
then and now, to recount,
or the business with Achitophel,
famous advisor, Kissinger-prototype,
or the matter of unfortunate, beautiful
Tamar, raped by one brother
revenged by another.
(But the worst part for her was how
Amnon loathed her after,
how he turned her out bolting his door,
how she wept and rent her
virgin's robes and cast ashes on her head...)
Let the family chroniclers all
make clear, how the nation
watched like sleepy spectators
at a summertime air show
thrilled by a dazzling daredevil
stunt that suddenly left them killed.

Because all I wanted to do was
write an elegy for Uriah, the Hittite.
I don't think much about Hittites
normally but Browning was on my mind
and my poem began, like this:
*"In the springtime of the year,*
*the time when kings go off to battle..."*
but then I realized those lines
were already in Second Samuel,
which is, isn't it?, always the way,
and besides, I couldn't work in when
David instructed Joab, "Send me Uriah,
the Hittite."
                (This line is very ominous,
right out of *The Godfather*, not the book
either, because what David intends
to do is kill Uriah, after having spied
on Bathsheba, the wife, as she bathed
on the roof next door, and having
summoned her to his royal quarters,
where in no Biblical time at all,
pretty much conveniently offstage
they apparently fell in love.
I find "Send me Uriah, the Hittite"
the second or third saddest line
ever, right after "Tell Michael it was
nothing personal"—*Godfather* again—or
Browning's Porphyria's Lover, who says
sweetly, absently, "I found a thing to do,"
referring to winding the hair three times
around the neck of a rich woman he loves
but cannot do anything short of
a fairly serious murder to keep.)

But along about this time, I grew
wary, convinced I would have to bring in
too much explanatory background
(unless the elegy got into the Norton,
and I could use my own footnotes…).
In any case, I would have to make clear
how David needed to seduce Uriah himself,
by making him, fresh and bloodied
from the battle with the Ammonites
(another people like us lost in time),
report to his own house and wash his feet
(David's strict and probably altogether
unpeculiar instruction for the time)
so that the king could make a credible case
that the baby who would someday be born
to Bathsheba could just possibly be
Uriah's own. Why David even poured
the good stuff to get the soldier in the mood.
But today who would not suspect this ploy?
And here's the most curious part of all:
Uriah, loyal Uriah, who routinely risked
his life for David on the battlefield,
tonight would defy his king.
He left David's holy presence and camped
all night outside the booths that housed
the ark of the covenant instead
and slept with his soldiers
and never went to Bathsheba's (euphemistic)
side.
When David found out next morning,
he knew a man this clever or this pure
or this dumb must be killed,
which authorities have always known,

and this is when he said, "Send me..." etc.,
though I bet there's some scroll from
the Dead Sea that goes into greater detail,
with David saying, "He did what...?"
All we know for sure is that now
Joab summarily isolated Uriah
in the fray and allowed him to be killed
by a stone an Ammonite woman flung
from the besieged walls of Rabbah,
and David's communications office could
maintain conveniently a posture
of plausible, upright deniability.

Maybe I should have, speaking of
Browning, written it from Uriah's
pathetic point of view—but that's the whole
problem, I don't think the man had one,
a distinct point of view. Sometimes love
destroys a man's imagination, and
sometimes it's the other way around.
Uriah simply saw what he could see,
Uriah did what he could do—and that's
the mystery of betrayals like this:
they're so ordinary, utterly.
The betrayed is betrayed first of all
by the essential fact he is incidental.
And my theory is that, like all
the betrayed, Uriah always always knew.
*(People had been stopping him*
*in Jerusalem, shocked by his sallow*
*face, asking what happened to his sense*
*of humor, asking what's wrong,*
*as he stumbled against the wells*

*and talked to himself*
*and blanched at their questions*
*as to how was Bathsheba and*
*when should they block out time*
*for an expected invitation to a bris.*
*He had tsuris before he could*
*explain why. In another age, he might*
*have joined a support group, got a*
*good lawyer, written essays,*
*taken up tai chi, aerobics, dope, or gin.)*
That last night he refused to go home
and look into the eyes of Bathsheba,
his wife who'd have to lie.
That last night I figure he barely slept
and readied himself to accommodate
David's and Bathsheba's and God's holy will.
It doesn't matter much I suppose, since
Uriah's case was lost since his first date
with the daughter of Eliam, he was a goner
from the first time Bathsheba stroked
his beard, he was expendable from the time
he was recruited for David's elite.
So when David sent for him,
Uriah simply went, understanding if not
knowing that he was already dead
for about three thousand years
and that desire is a terrible, terrible
thing for a man who is not involved
and that murder and desire for another man's
wife are absolutely intertwined.
If you don't believe Uriah or this poem,
there's a book he and I would recommend.

## Poem in which he writes the last poem in which:

The summer death's terror
was casually displaced,
the old dog we loved took
to walking into closed doors,
standing in the sun, staring
with eyes spooling into space.
Then she'd burrow into sleep
as if sleep were a cave where
the interesting bones were hid.
Later, she'd turn from her bowl
and listen to hovering bees.
We placed her under the shade
between our two maple trees.
Whole centuries believed.
And still the old news stuns
when the phone rings,
the middle of the night.
Our voices are the ones that break.
We dress ourselves in the dark.
We're driving somewhere before we think.

## Poem in which a vision is recalled:

We were thirty rungs high in the chapel tower
while the country conducted a religious war.
That night, we had a vision—of Jack Daniels.
And revealed before us was The Miracle of
the Cracked Ice. Still, something more—or something
else—surged with us past the midnight rooms,
compelled us through the white gold chapel,
hopelessly lifting us up the creaky ladder to
the top of the spire that none of us risked ascending before.
In grape-crushing time, catching our breath
in the resinous, chewy breeze coming off the lake,
we remarked on the high beams heading for town.

From up there, I saw the deer finesse
the vines with tenuous, postoperative tenderness.
And probably the night probably passed. Then
something like a tide reversed, and something
like shooting stars differently fell,
and something like rumors confused all the trees.
Here I was, close to heaven as I'd ever be,
a citizen of the next and a stranger in this
and in all worlds to be redeemed.

# *WIT'S END*

*I have had a most rare vision. I have had a dream, past the wit of man to say what dream it was. Man is but an ass, if he go about to expound this dream. Methought I was—there is no man can tell what. Methought I was—and methought I had—but man is put a patched fool if he will offer to say what methought I had. The eye of man hath not heard, the ear of man hath not seen, man's hand is not able to taste, his tongue to conceive, nor his heart to report, what my dream was.*

—A Midsummer Night's Dream

# PART ONE: OCCASIONS

*"I, who boast of embracing the pleasures of life so assiduously and so particularly, find in them, when I look at them thus minutely, virtually nothing but wind. But what of it? We are all wind. And even the wind, more wisely than we, loves to make a noise and move about, and is content with its own functions, without wishing for stability and solidity, qualities that do not belong to it."*

—Montaigne

# OCCASION OF STRANGERS

When we at last meet, as of course we must,
You will recognize me by my firebird
That pecks continually on my lapel.
And you, whom I've never known, how could I
Forget your jeweled quiver, your otter fur cape?

At the party, after the play, on the moon,
I meet you saying, "Isn't Kandinsky a bore?
What's your favorite Russian novel?
Have you really saved the elephants?
How long have you played that tremendous oboe!"

When I ask for your name, please take your cue:
Ask for mine. Forget it the moment I say it.
In turn I will gladly do the same for you.
Now comes the hard part: we must be unencumbered
By any sense of communion. You should be married.

I am happily divorced. I live with six cats
And you're allergic. I want to be certain that
You get the picture: we truly are engaged
In dissimilar pursuits—you work for
The diplomatic corps while I'm in Byzantine Lit.

Religious views conveniently contradict:
I'll have a clean body coming from the hearses,

You'll be the swaying udder of a cow.
I notice your mole, you watch my repaired teeth.
I see I'll need to make more conversation.

"In my spare time I am an astronaut,
My father's the president of G.M., after school
I swallowed fire at the circus. Yawning, you lean
Over, spill your drink, confess, "I love to eat
Sweetbreads and shave my legs when I'm high."

Suddenly we are the only ones left at the bar,
At the party, in the craters. This is the time
To be discreet. *I have never met anyone
Like you.* You say: "I am an old chair, an empty
Cut glass vase, a gold ring lost in the gutter."

Taking you to my house, I tell you, that's all right.
I am vacated rooms, white roses, the severed hand.
We are words placed perfect on the sheet.
Every time after the occasion of strangers, I profess
New theories for their consummate sadness.

# FOR MY CONTRACEPTED CHILDREN

Where have you not been for so long?
We did not worry for you. We did
Not call up any of your friends.
Now finally today you come home
With nothing in your arms as gift
For me, with no arms to bear gifts,
Without even coming back at all.
You have not been playing in the park
All day, your knees are not scraped.
You do not want anything at all
For your birthday. If you asked
Me about Santa Claus I could
Lie with a clean conscience. You
Are not curious about mommy
And where she is and it is better
That way. When you seem puzzled
Or anxious, and I worry about it,
Nothing's your reply. Sit around
Me now, I'll tell you no story.
No dreams enfold the wings you
Feel capable of on your back.
At least the night does not shake
Your neck with its cold fingers.
At least you will not fall in love
And be bored and think about things.
And you won't become disappointed

In us all, because we've tried—
As best we could—to take care of
Everything for you, to free you from
The blind date who doesn't show,
The wild pitch that lost the game.
We tried to ungive you the whole world.

# OBJET D'ART

Disinterested, they come to see me,
Something unique, the experts claim.
Saint Jerome kept me on his table,
Or I surfaced from a Nantucket grave.
I was the vial of poison in the Pharoah's
Tomb. I sliced up the tribal meals.
I am the fading sketch of something
Inarticulate—perhaps the view from
Mont Blanc, Everest, or Abora,
Perhaps the shade of the trees along
The Rhine. I am the most fragile
Sculpture I conceive—the teeth
Of a shaman or an ivory amulet.
The circlet of dull hair around
The bone. Maybe the scroll urging
The country to war, ordering the king
Beheaded, dissolving a church or two—
Crumbling under glass. Shut are
The visors of the helmets of knights.
The cannon point away, distantly,
Colonial. Even the guards are
Asleep. All the insurance has expired.
There is nothing can protect me now:
The friendly man in dark glasses and skinny tie,
Sharp pocket knife and a hammer inside.

# DRUNKEN CONVERSATION

When you talk to me I want to take refuge
In my classical grammars, trying to establish
Precedent for this new syntactical arrangement.
No doubt this is a conditional clause, my mood
Indicative, yours outrageously subjunctive.
Christ, your cuneiform is flawless, but my carbon
14 is in low supply.

                            In the cave where we lived
Ten thousand years ago surely it was simpler.
You must recall the finger paintings by torch light
—the hours we spent depicting the beasts on
The cave walls, the tamed dog suddenly at our feet,
Club in my grasp, the rows of corn and hut we called
Home.

               I need to put this historical event
In its cultural context, establish the text,
Verify your article's veracity.

                                 I just keep
Coming down the mountain with stones in my arms,
And there you dance in firelight, your body tattooed
Red and gold, your hair greased with pig fat, and
Your hands reach for as several eons
Worth of ice begin to melt. An entire ocean
Comes between us.

                        The bar is closing.

# FLIGHT

Who would know the flight my desperation took
Till I clicked my heels and prayed:
Fly this 707 to Oz,
There's no place like Om.

I rehearse it all for weeks, trying it out on everyone.
I tell my wife, To Oz! She says, I love you, too.
I tell my teacher, Take me to Oz!
He explains pathetic fallacy,
The figures of speech: synecdoche, simile,
Misery.
At last I resort to the dog, whose name is Oz.
I chant, like a question, in his grimy ear,
To know how sudden all affection soon lapses.

Unnoticed all the way to the cabin door,
I've lost my composure, so I try to assure them:
I insist to myself I am sane,
But I find myself telling them:

Give me a million. Take me to Miami.
I want to die simply in the sun.

# MY FATHER DECLARES BANKRUPTCY

Three days after Christmas and
A court concedes to you your life's
Achievement. How many times
Did you just

               miss the big money?
Put money to win and show instead?
Ride the odds to come up even?
Take the week-

               end up at Stateline,
Get shuffled like a card under tables?
I once dreamed I was the dealer
To the whole

               family. My cards would
Fly with smiling precision in the plum-
Colored sky at sunset. I meant to say,
I suppose,

               despite everything, I tried
To love you. But here you are, fifty,
Your wife and sons who left you.
Behind you is

               a New York, left to try
A California. The finance companies
Plot in their granite buildings to
Confiscate

               all your possessions,
As if that ever really mattered.

And it might be funny were it not
So damned
                inevitable. Flat on the face
Of it your expenses exceeded your
Assets, and what's worse, even the hope
Of any assets.
                        I notice my name
Is missing from the list of creditors.
How much do I owe? What court can settle
Our accounts?

# PHILOSOPHY 1-A:
# THE WISDOM OF THE WEST

*We are not as wretched, as we are worthless.*
—Montaigne

Fresh off the theories of inefficiency, impotence,
Causes, lungs converting exhaust, of Stork and of Oz,
Of vitamin pills and yogurt, my body out there
Humming with secret dark computations of intestines,
Glands and heart, I am dying, Montaigne, dying,
From radiation or from trying, and credo quia
I feel all right.

                And once I dreamt I shouted to
The world—Cork! And the Teacher replied, Profound!
This is the most finite repetition of the infinite I-
Am—you cannot keep a good cork down.

                                  Sum

Ergo sum, and how to demonstrate it? Cogito?
Ambulo? Scripto? Stupro? There is a certain
Point from which there is no return. This is
Kafka's assumption. Yesterday was epiphany.
And now we have the naming of parts. Which
We have not got. Not even in the Black Holes
Of South Dakota and the Universe. And some-
Where in infinite or in San Diego innumerable
Monkeys peck away at the keyboard keys—
Writing Shakespeare, Swinburne, and the Sporting
Green. This is positively negative capability.
And I want to be like them because I spin and

Spoil everything. Poor Narcissus for taking cheap
Advice—not everyone should know himself so well.
This is the function of criticism, and as old Chesterton
Said, the criticism of function.
                              Of America
          I sing, her free clinics, Disneyland, and Nixon.
And out of the classrooms endlessly talking,
Endlessly, endlessly, I have come too late for
The gods, a lifetime too early for graduate credit.
There is a real stone and a real world in here
And out there because it was kicked empirically
Out of the way.

                    Logically speaking, we're in trouble.
Ax mark in The Theoretical Speculation. *Check.*
The powdered wig on The Subjective A Priori. *Check.*
The campfire of what we are saying extinguished.
*Check.* And no birds sing. (Tragic biographical
Footnote.) *Check.* The music of the spheres as
The Objective Correlative. *Check.* The abandoned
Watchtower. *Check.* Gutted school building. *Check.*
Flying castle. *Check and check again.*
                              I have arrived.

*PERFECT SPIRITUAL TWENTY-THREE-YEAR-OLD MASTER*

You cannot put the foot in
The same mouth twice. Aum. Aum.
Take off the clothes forever, this
Is transcendence. Aum. Aum.
Being in the world is a full-time
Occupation. Aum. Aum.
Never unexpect the unexpected.
Aum. Aum. Aum.

# SORROW

I would rather watch the rain come down.
But I do not mean the rain,
I mean the staccato of the invisible sun
Sucked bead by bead from the ground.
And there's nothing worth saying,
Except that. And nothing left to do
But wait for all the scientists
Certain to arrive. Turned inside to the place
Where every seam shows, all my glands
On my sleeve, watching the blood
Rush through my heart, watching
The fibers knitting up bones, I lament
Each enzyme doing perfunctory work,
I grieve for my kidneys' efficiency,
And see cigar smoke do a great job
Of making brass rubbings of my lungs.
They'll come like archaeologists,
Shoveling out of me the language,
Unearthing all my ancient artifacts
Of past lives, celebrating the findings
Of multi-leveled soils, turning over
Painted cisterns of stagnant water,
Searching somewhere for the tip of a spire.

# A NOTE ON RECONCILIATION

All the ink in all the letters we have written and will write
Is becoming blue luminous, fresh once more and wet,
Each letter is just about to appear on the page
Or, just drawn, is ready to evaporate in the air
We come up to breathe, the air in which our words bathe.

Alone, by this cold light, on this flat surface,
I take my pen and pull myself back through each word
And inside the body our old inks form new patterns,
Blend a different color, the need to recall the date
I've erased and left the clumsy salutation intact.

For two years in my drawer your letters waited
And when today I looked I found them bleached
Of what time does to deny a blank page brightness.

And yet the shadows lingered everywhere in the words.
I felt the late afternoon shudder, I heard the small bell
Of ice in your glass, it was all I could do to write this down.

# THE SON'S POEM

Twenty years later still
I am the one good coat
From your closet of moths,
Useful on cold winter mornings,
During the long nights of water.

One time something went wrong
In the cellar. Mother said
You were working on the furnace.
It was snowing and the radio said
Another storm was coming.
When you came back upstairs,
Your fingers bleeding slightly
From their blued tips, you took
Me to your chest, and I slept.

As a coat, I know a little
Of those dark countries,
The closet and the suitcase.
All day—all ways, all time
—I am in use, firmly
Upon your shoulders.

Elbow patches frayed,
Cuffs too, buttons loose or lost,
I am the burden of your aging back,
The source of your warmth.

What is so difficult
To learn is what I must
Show you: in summer
One goes without me,
But you can count on our
Being together in the end.

# WORKING IN THE IDEA OF A GARDEN

Take the early morning cold,
For instance, around six,
In the idea of a garden
It is March of course.

Everything is clothed by
A small ring of crispest silver.
All the subtle ground is sillion,
Bright as the long lettuce leaves.
The opulence of eucalyptus,
Jasmine flower blooming,
There is a wide banner
In the air the color of tomato.
The white blossom which is the surfeit
Of lemon trees and more lemon trees.
The happy corpulence of avocado.

Certainly weeds multiply, the slugs
And snails dominate the earth,
The hornets soon to be out
In their vengeful air—
But this is the work of
The long afternoon, the thought
Before sleep.
And now the sun is soon to arrive.
It is making itself known

By degrees fathomable to us
Working in the idea of a garden.

By degrees fathomable to us
Working in the idea of a garden.

# THE DUMB PAGE

You who pretend so perfectly to nothingness
Are much too clever for my moored reflections
Less evanescent, as they are, than a docked and peeling
Rowboat, it being midnight, and the moon,
It being less than half itself.

A message? That's it? Cable? Tele? Candy? What?
What have you to say to me, Christ, it could never
Be the Delphic one, my phone's been off for weeks.
Will you sing it? Dance it? Speak it with a soft
Voice? Orchestrate your arms to feign intent?

Your profession! What you *have* to say
Matters infinitely less than what certainly *is*,
You are chance, you are certainty.
Certainly, chances I take with you mean more
Than a blind chip lost and blue in Reno.

If only to have initially imagined you
Finally, to have given you milk and blood,
Given you shelter and chair, portrait
And memory. But this is no excuse, I think:
The last word I leave you with: this is all there is.

The word will come in the morning.
I will study you like a heartbroken lover,

Say, "You've been translated. What was reality
Is now forever dream. I am content."
Even ink acquires the color of seeming purpose. Why not you?

You who pretend to nothingness are surely everything.
My fingers are certain to obey you,
Such, the power of night,
Such, the melodies making their moist way
Up throat and rocketing off the tongue.

# LOVE SONG OF THE ID

My dark my fluent hondo!
Howsoever you go, I'll follow.

I fed you the sweetness of my palm,
Read you Augustine and Henry James,
Spoke well of you (mostly) to friends.
But in school each time you let me down
In different rooms each night. I sought
Special friends for you in magazines,
Zoos, the streets. At least, I begged you,
Be discreet, don't defecate on my name.

But at night I know you in despair,
I can feel my foundation shake.
I can hear you limp on the stairs,
Until, in every dream, in you barge—
Large as life and living. Large.
I have to forgive your appetite.

Now no matter what, what new tack
I take, what grunted agreements we make,
You think the whole world tastes sweet.
And I know I cannot keep you chained,
I know that when I fall asleep
You wander, crashing through the gates,
Moaning all night for candy, for meat.

# MAN WITH GESTURES

After his career as athlete,
Or magician, or admin.ass't,
He can wave a kind word at you
With a professional kind of grace.
Plans and extravagant proposals
Exude from his forearms and chest.
He walks on his eyes and hands.

In his lassitude such a man stares
Out hoping at the other end of things,
Perhaps, he will see the back of his head,
And turning around give a wink.

The man with gestures has two
Children and he has a wife.
Each morning he kisses them Good Morning.
Each evening he kisses them Good Night.

One day a man with gestures raised
His hands to the ceiling and with a face
Blank past sadness
He smiled.
      At some point he died. Other men
Of gestures buried him. We could
Not get away to be there.
We sent a card.
We left flowers.

# MEA CULPA
## FOR MY LIFE IN SYRACUSE

*for L.B.*

-1-
When you wonder who
Lets the air from your tires,
Or who puts the wormy
Apple on your desk,
Or who persuaded your
First grader to piss in his seat,
Know that it is me.

At night when you
Awaken from the odd
Recurring dream of some
Strange man singing off-
Key and too loudly in public
Places and you rush
Happily to your door, please
Do not be glad. No one
Is there, it is me.

-2-
One morning your circus
Arrived. Though I looked
Forward to it, I was still

Surprised. Banners! Carriages!
Elephants! The mustachioed
Woman who lifted a cow!
The drums with the trumpets,
The frivolous pipe organ!

Without need of a reason,
I confess, that night I set fire
To the big-top tent and nearby
Watched as the frantic red
Trucks struggled.
In your confusion I unleashed
The tigers and the bears.
I fed the lions your clowns.
I led your barkers and
Ticket sellers to
The cages of gorillas.

And that spectacular attraction
Of yours, a dazzling fleet of
Flamingoes, I by night,
By the angry light
Of acetylene torch, I
Poisoned their food, their water.
And while you looked down
The window I convinced
You to climb to,
It was me—I carried
The blue ladder away,
I sold the stairs at a profit.

# DOUBLE FEATURE

*For my brothers who took me*

The last herd of buffalo has stampeded
Into the last dark grey sunset, and
Every hero has turned out human.
Even Hopalong got old, kicked the bucket.
But I have not forgotten the dark of
The Winthrop, the aisles teeming with
Flesh shadows and flashlights, the smell
Of popcorn and the sensation of my teeth
Going very bad in my mouth with candy.
The eagle comes to roost on the earth
Of celluloid and old Gene stars smooching
His Amanda closedmouth and teethlessly,
As she sits on the porch of her very white house.
Later, after rounding up all of the black-
Hats, he wonders about another chance
With her on her porch as he consults
With the grizzly old-timer, polishing
His pearl-handle pistols, unconscious
Or secretive in the knowledge that
Prairie bush was moving alive with Indians.
And then it all changes:
                              The scaly fish/man
Monster still possesses the native indiscretion
To desire the beautiful, brainy, blonde

Ichthyologist, and leave her impotent
Intended scientist knocked out on
The experimental floor. With her, the monster
Climbs up to the roller coaster top,
Having passed unnoticed along New York
Thoroughfares, bearing her in shock in his arms/
Fins all the way to the Palisades Park.
And while the toy tanks set their sights,
And the hundreds of mini-soldiers prepare to
"Blow it to Kingdom Come soon as I
Grab the babe!" he looks out to them all,
Pleading and uncomprehending. Then,
Just before a gillion million volts traverse
The tracks to his organic flippers,
He cries out something we all understand
In our very own strange and monster tongue.
(*Darkness.*)                    (*Very dim lighting.*)

# 28 JUNE 1973

Asleep, you
Are a museum after the wars

A sunlit tapestry
Draped over a formation of stone

A clean hand
Lying next to an important

Impressionist
A flower vase on the fields of

Dandelions
A woman with a basket of fruit

At the foot of
A woman with a basket of fruit.

# LOVE SONG OF THE VAMPIRE

Do not plead for reasons when I am upon you.
I am your impossible night window
Opened by the wind. I am your loveliness
Blooming, brushing your pale cheeks damask.
I've come in your deepest sleep, because I must,
Carried by the wings of the small dark twitching
Blind animal that flies inside of you,
Love. So close to you, I am the air you gasp
To breathe, the nervous lump of your pulsating
Throat. And if we do not speak, celebrate how,
Wordless, we can hold whatever secrets we are.
The kiss, so final, so deep, when we part is all
That matters where you know me in this dark world.
I curse the sun that keeps you oblivious away,
Jealous of your day-to-day life, though I know
Daylight defends you, as it hides me, from what
Your opening eyes would not dare recognize.

# TO THE MAN WHO WAS NOT

Each morning as my eyes open
I bring my death back to life.
But it never used to be:
There were meadows and mountains and snow,
And it's been the same since I remember.
My sight funnels into the room:

My vision drops into those chutes,
The private passageways to things:
Driftwood, amulet, and fireplace,
Birdcage, tapestry, chair.
It never used to be, like this, or this.

I've become the boat that will not reach port,
The pebble dropped off the cliff,
At low ebb a tidepool. Forgive me,
Death, my reluctance: at the party,
In the catacombs, above the cathedral,
Lying beneath the lemon trees.

I greet you tapping presciently on
The xylophone of my spine, tutor of
The nameless hooded instructors—hawk
Flight, shark bait, the halved moon.
In your eye, your singlest eye,
A cracked monocle. Mathematician
To the zero power, minus one, me.

# THE MOMENT

It never happened or it would always be,
The moment.
The savagery, spectacle, the ardor—
Surreal as history.
We found the mask on fire and meant
To leave ourselves swinging open like a door.

The mask was in place, ephemeral, entire,
When the gods came
On the ocean and love's myth vanished
Like the froth. After fire
Nothing can be the same.
As it is. Before the day blinked, astonished,

Closed, on the tarred and extending shore,
A snowy egret rose
Up into the air to fly circles in the rain:
Civilized and bored
We saw the distant crows
On the trestle, listened in silence to the train.

# OPEN HEART SURGERY

They found me propped straight in the corner
Of my room. I had given up therapies for good,
Nothing would stop the calcifying endgame.

Each day I grew more detached, sentimental.
The sunset could make we weep, the album
Of photographs forced me a week into the house.

When they came for me at last, the knock
At the door, before they burst in, sounded far off,
Not possible, a voice from a deeper gorge.

I lapsed and woke to see the surgeon, green as
A mantis, with his hands rip open my chest.
He saw the crazy spectacle of my heart:

The rampaging elephants through an African
Village, the rives overflowing. A child
Wide-eyed in the theater balcony watching

The same projections over and over.
Triumphant, the doctor seems to have found it:
The secret trying to slide away under the seat,

Then hanging slippery from the chandelier,
Posing as the usher, as the forgotten villain.
In his hands, bloody, it begins to squirm,

But he puts it up to my eyes. I see. My eyes
Clear. I laugh it to scorn. Everyone laughs.
All these scars would testify.

## STARLIKE

You know how it is.
You start one day to ignore
The panhandlers and their tin cups,
The children in wheelchairs,
The old woman who stumbles,
The man flailing the air.

You remain content anyway,
Reading the paper calmly and
Voting and sleeping alone and
Sometimes with another; you are
Humiliated by the accidents
You come across on the way.

Someone looks at you passing by,
You drink a good wine, hear
Your favorite symphony. You think
One day you fall in love
And discuss with her
Raising a family, which ceremony.

Now and then you plan
To go to church and acknowledge
It all. You know how it is.
And then it happens.
Something starlike enters you
While waking.

You have disciplined
Yourself to expect nothing, or
Only a little. Suddenly,
Everything is offered and
Nothing suffices. You have given
Dominion back to the world.

The world ignores your gift.
You resign yourself to your
Limitations. The ocean
Mocks you. You tell yourself,
I'm free. A cabdriver says,
Where to? You know how it is.

But then this morning something
Starlike enters you while
You creep in the wilderness
Between sleep and wakefulness.
Everything telescopes.
A star is sent from a great distance.

Suddenly in your eye you see.
It is this kind of seeing.
The beggar is in your heart,
The deaf and mute are in your soul.
You look at your family at dinner,
Only see the wounded and apologize.

A moth flutters around your
Nightlight and you weep.
You have hated God and lived
Alone for years. You know how it
Is. This morning in this
Bed you recall your birth.

A light comes to you, still, unmasking,
Forgiving, to wake you and all
The faces and voices you are.
This must be a baptism
Because you grow
Thankful and beg of everyone—

Your father and mother,
Your friends and enemies,
The house you were born in, the mountain
And the sparrow, the dogs,
Your wife and your sons—
If you might please exist.

# PART TWO: ESSAYS

*"If my mind could gain a firm footing, I would not make essays, I would make decisions."*
—Montaigne.

# THE BEAUTIFUL WOUNDS

The leper in a cathedral knows all too well
How deeply the beautiful wounds.
The blind man who regains his eyes at forty
Knows that sunlight is a beautiful scar
Upon the darkness he learned to prefer.
Even the vines trellised and constrained
Give their fruit in the chaos of controlled
Agony. A tree like the mind planting it
Cuts the earth with a beautiful wound.
The spider webs like the man unfolding
His strange string of life glistens
In a true light like a beautiful wound,
For the beautiful wounds. The carpenter's
Secret table, the eyes going deeper,
And the beautiful wounds. The pictures
Coming back out of focus, confused, occasions
Of strangers, the uterus of delusion.
The white marble kissing the cold body
Of dying, the stonecutter inhaling dust.
The sad man walks out without wondering,
Telling the Mardi Gras of gnomes and lepers
To join him by rivers to be christened,
To laugh with him for the beautiful wounds.

# ESSAY ON LOVE

*Stinson Beach, 1975*

*One*

Wherever it is I find you
I am always in the doorway
Standing sidelong looking down
Unable to go away, unwilling

To face the camera, the music,
Unwilling to come in. Where could I go.
My clothes turn animal again
The rose of the wood flowers into gardens,

Your tears a river we seek for the source.

*Two*

Such intimate coalescence: who & what
We are standing in the door. Now
In this moment the bondage of molecules
Is a simple mockery of us,

Wing tissue tearing audibly in the night,
No word would suffice. It's so like a circle
I stand still perfectly to cross over.
Reflections confirm motives. We've touched

Bottom and seek a greater depth.

*Three*

The rivers carry me to oceans
That would wash the past of me:
The long sonorous refusals of the shore,
The jagged-edged accountancies

Of the shell. I cannot help but envy
All the sleek swimmers
Changed by wishing to be dolphins and seals.
That morning I found myself like mist

On the ground waiting for the dissipated
Sun, these nights I walk the coast
Listening for the creaks in the wrecks
Of my imagination, licking the salt

From the plum-dark sky. I've wished
To look into the distance and watch
The drowned thrash their bodies
In the glow of my misunderstanding.

Something tells me there must have been
A moment when you did not exist.
I do not know. I cannot say for sure.
I have practiced in my room and just walking

The shore to hold my breath and breathe.

*Four*

I have through my history revealed
An ignorance more to myself than
I know and still stood like Doric
Purposeless columns mitigated

By a wind which would level me
One day, would take me to a land
Unknown to myself. Nothing, no
One can heal me, now a lament

Seizes the orchestras of guitars,
Lyres, and harps and yet my song
Dies like a weak bird in the copse
Like a sandpiper under the wheel.

My heart is the monument to
Uncivil wars, a map emblazoned
With the succession of storied
Losses and penultimate victories.

Defeated and unholy I would reach
Out for you in the world
Defeated and unholy, sing a song so
Fleeting, perfect, and defiled no one could

Hear me, no one could heal me but you.

*Five*
We may not survive the night.
We are too solemn for the moon
And we close our curtains.
How curious is it, the fall

Into you wrapped savagely by sleep.
How could we survive all of this?
Tortured planets malign us,
A contingency of orbit

Frees us to keep spinning beyond
Any impossible certainty
The way our fig trees
Blossomed falsely Indian summer

But then the cold and rains came
And seeds died all over the ground.
Sometimes we can barely lift
Each other up, raise the water cup

To our lips. In the fireplace
We turn over the ashes of a hundred letters,
A hundred times we tried to find words.
Tonight I keep opening the door

Letting the wind rush through our house.

*Six*
Inside beyond the cemetery
Of epitaphs to myself, beyond resolutions
To change and adhere
Plainly, inhere in the towers of hope

I feel a graver weight than
Gravity, a pressure lighter than
Air. I would give it your name
But I would not give it your voice.

I feel myself in particles of light
Rushing past space into
A time we can survive. Today
I walked into the forest

And into myself, a vacuum,
Suddenly I constructed formlessness
And my house shook free of itself:
I walked out. Such an ocean,

Such a whiteness and an ocean,
And there came from it everyone
We loved so perfect in such costume
The lights like prisms fracturing

My vision, I wept into so many pieces.

*Seven*
And what if we should one day
Begin to yield
Bravely ask a question creviced like a bowl
And find it empty at the bottom

And if we should some day
Wake up to nothing
We'd dare recognize and nonetheless survive:
Pass beyond the saddest shorelines we could plot

And what if we should
Turn away, say goodbye,
Cling to the inside of this cracked bell of a word,
And toll to deafness our whole mind

Let us suppose we could
Come inside the rain to hear
The house echo from without to watch ourselves
Yield    dare    wake    achieve

The perfect mastery of this
Instant hollowed out like your mouth opened
To ask if we had become
Empty of even this, this question,

One day what if we should?

*Eight*
I heard the cry of foghorns just now
In the middle of a clear afternoon.
Never again will I take for granted
The sun, never be mindless in human weathers.

What could, what could not
Threaten the intimate circumference of this light?
Somewhere off the coast arrives
The rain, inarticulate rushes of wings

A sudden downpour keep me quiet
Near you. I can observe strictly
Nothing you do not love
Or do. I am beginning

To know nothing for the first time again.

# NEGLIGIBLE

After I pack up my things and stick a pin
In our waterbed I would leave you. Go on,
Laugh. Laugh. But you'd know right away
Something had gone wrong. You'd start buying
Your own cigarettes—what is it, two packs a day
Now? Whose coffee left on the table for a week
Would you spill out? Your neurotic cat
Would abandon you or would sit on the piano
For a month. Things would be suddenly different,
Radically. Radically. You would go through the rooms
With your vacuum, alone, and every single night
Would be forced to think up a meal. We tried
To share responsibilities, at first, remember?
Something down in your back would pop when
You were reaching up for your big box store
Dishware on the higher shelves. I took mine along.
I've got the wine glasses, too, use your goblets,
You're drinking too much anyway.

It would not hit you really until you grew tired.
Then who would you ask at my desk—
What are you working on?—in that sultry, fake
Movie star voice. You would have to invite the man
From work, or the man from the Christmas party,
Or the man from your phony reading group, or
Your grocer, or your God-damned psychotherapist—

Anyone, anyone at all I guess, to convince him
That it would wait until tomorrow.


But let me not to the marriage of untrue minds
Admit the truth of impediment. You hated literary
Allusions. That's why I've left you my Russian novels,
You would like them. One night, after sipping my cognac,
Take one down and sit in your chair by the fire.
You will turn to my bookmark and wonder why I stopped
Reading there:
               The sled coming down the estate,
The horses in red blankets and jangling their bells
As the snow keeps falling and falling. Why turn the page
With a hero?
               His family is gone—his young wife
And their only son—his father will not spare him the news.
He will never leave his home for the war again.
He will set aside one room for her special chair,
Her water colors.
               And your eyes want merely to
Close. Your grasp on things…going nowhere.
You jump at the sound of something crashing down in
Your house. But return, like a soldier, to the bells' fading
Sound, and turn for the warmth of the radiant snow
As, open, my book drops down into your lap.

# SURVIVOR

All the friends had given me up for lost.
I hear how I'd lived to return from you frozen
Beneath myself, how against all odds, against
My own nature, I chose to resist, to survive.

For a few days I managed by feasting on sweetness
I remembered, but his source was shallow
And was too soon depleted. Those appetites
I acquired from you which never could be sated.

Coming back your face loomed from the clouds.
I imagined you in the oasis, your men feeding you grapes,
Drinking white wine.
                                        I always felt you behind me
Filming what you'd term my escape, for the record.
Waving my arms I could attract no other's attention.
So I continued. All the friends flew overhead
Blithe reconnaissance missions. I continued on.

All the maps proved worthless, precise. Nothing I'd learned
Showed me where you begin, where it was you left me,
Where I had to go.
                                In barren, darkened lands,
In the singed meadows I listened with care to
The vacancies of birdsong, watched the elusive
Absence of possum bear, deer, and butterfly.

I drank deeply from the crags my thirst.
From the height of the fruit trees fell my hunger.

Once, once only, I was tempted. I took to my mouth
My hand and hit into the flesh.
It tasted of nothing so much as it did of you.

I resisted sitting down to die in the ruins
Of what I piloted into the mountain.
At the moment of impact I knew that
The mountain had been worth it,
And the beautiful, beautiful crash,
The absolute cold that leveled me
Into my senses, the snow falling
To deliver me lastly to the ledge
Where you left me and we left each other.

# MEDITATION ON THE ANGELS

*For Josephine Miles*

All year long survives a season
When knowing itself seems to know:
A kind of radical summer when oranges
Demand praise for illuminating
Symmetry by their confident pose on the table;
I mean affection considered as permanent
Occasion, as everlastingness of clear weather.
It occurs when people wear lesser clothes.

Any momentary interlude: awareness
Of the moment in its passing. The girl
Weeping helplessly by the window,
The auctioning of a trunk of letters;
The revolver dropped to the floor,
Cartridge shells empty as boats back
From a cruise on the Ganges; the black swan
Floating on the palace moat.

How many failed, sick, ambitious
Angels would dance on the head of a pin?
Give thanks our angels are unnecessary.
The obsolescent hunters of unicorns.
Nobel Prize-winning pioneers of black holes.
Fashioners of Faery Land and Arcadia.

The lantern seen through the caboose window.
The last lighthouse operator on the coast.

The heart, the rational but stupid heart,
Summons like the realms of the angels,
Their faint signals growing dim, like stars
Lapsing in this universe to stream in
The mind of quite some other. What shall we
Say in the absence? (My voice trails away.
I can these days hardly carry a tune,
And there is no dance, no clearing, no

Circle.)          *Anymore*. Perhaps
We may know too much. But I left my bed
To go outside at dawn down to the lake that froze
Over in the night. I needed to taste the coldest
Water and I smashed my fist through the ice.
Holding one sliver of it up to the sun—
Shimmering against the sky, a host of angels
Singing like the wind in a chorus of trees.

# WHEN IT TAKES PLACE

It will not take place within the clearing
And the song of thrush and the whippoorwill
Will not fill up his head. Perhaps, the bark
Of the beached seal, the final cry of
The killer whale, maybe, knowing him, the howl
Of a white wolf up at the absent moon.

In the sky, and even above that, the memory
Of the stars, not the stars themselves; below,
The lake surface unfurling like forgotten lands'
Darkened flags. Before the planets will have crashed
The sun, he will be on his way, I mean else-
Where, to where after other journeys others arrived.

Once there he will learn, in his new language,
How to ask for water and not get a thing
In return, how to reach the station and be glad
When he loses direction, how to photograph
The air that parts behind him where he goes,
How to feign surprise for what keeps taking place.

He will, it goes without saying, not be alone:
All the parties will have fizzled out long before,
Long-distance runners will have turned forever
Their backs on destination's arbitrary dominion,
The music scores litter the way, stage lights
Glimmering, as instruments rust in constant rain.

It will be strange, the sensation that shines
Within, how this has transpired a thousand
Times for a thousand years. Even the October
Leaves will grin up at him from the apple-strewn
Ground, amazed at how the ladders stand tall
Up to the full trees without any rungs to climb.

He will read in the next day's paper of what
He failed to achieve, the names of the women
Who tried to care, the books he wrote now lost
In good friends' rooms. On his way there, where it
Will be impossible to care, nonetheless it will
Linger, regret, like dust in the midday air,

And he will await the sunset to clear the house.
After the fact, the children crying out in novels,
On the screen, will move him to a kind of smile:
His eyes will close and he'll stretch out to take in
Some little light at a time. There will be documents,
Elaborate attestations for the record, for which

There is no need of him. We will not be sure
When it is he arrives: one of us will check his pulse
And push open, this one last time, his eyes. We who
Tried all of our lifetimes to get to this point
Now see in at what he no longer wants to endure.
I will think of him as a mountain range, his body

In its final white relief under the white sheet.
Back in the world he forever wanted to love, things
Will be different. After the event, his dog will growl
On the floor, the calf in the slaughterhouse will
Drop, the squirrels will avoid his path, far away
Hungry bears will run from him catching the scent,

Each deer will headlong turn into the traffic
And two eagles will claw each other to death
For one lamb. I mean, it will go without any
Notice. We will give thanks for that at least,
The only grace given in the world we're given to know.
Looking down at him we will not know each other.

Someone will try to call him a good man, or great,
But we will shout him down in chorus to silence.
Now that he has arrived we will resist our wishing
To go along, the journey will appear less difficult, or
More, but, mending our shoes for the hundredth time, we
Will take to him the earth he hoped all along to survive.

# VERY DARK POEM

Between the toadstools, in this home-grown dark
I can locate myself barely, now that I've left the place
Of ash, dead leaf, mulch, and manure.
Perhaps, someday, I'll grow accustomed to it
And not resent the roots that implicate.

From this place that is nothing if not passing to substance,
I culture no interest in what the world provides,
Content, if tentative, with quotidian
Adjustments in my small place—some new snails,
My friendly aphids, surprising seeds and crabgrass.

I have grounded myself utterly in the dark plot
And no longer look for cosmic rearrangements among
My decadent clouds. Feel no pity for the decline
Of the sea. I have turned myself under a hundred times
For his wholly dark impermanence, my very dark poem.

# TEACHING THE CHILDREN

We are learning, all of us, Literature.
The Literature of the World Literature.

Today is Monday. Today is Tuesday.
If we let it, perhaps, today is Sunday.
I turn to the blackboard and look for
Shadows grimly dancing on the chalk tray.
Teaching Literature to Children. Of
The World. The sun comes out. Could
There be any question?

Say: Word. Now notice. Make oval your mouth.
Make it round as a funnel from which anything
Might arrive, round as a tunnel in darkness
And on the other side bright light. Keep
Your lips (word-saying) firm, as if something
Has taken your breath or frightened you
Terribly, but breathe, and be brave. As if
You had a fire in your presence, as if
A falcon flew to your black-gloved fist, as
If your finger touched a nipple, or the tip
Of a penis. Now let your mouth have rest,
Let its tongue fall upward to the bottom,
The roof, and have it all end, and without
Ending, end it, still saying for all the world
To hear, Word Word Word Word Word.

These are words. They will grow friendly in
Time with you, but do not be anxious
Over them. You know how you feel a horse?
You know how to ice-skate? It is all the same.
Listen. Billy has words, so has Sally.
And also Melvin, and Virginia and Gino,
And Sarah, and poor Andrew, who stutters, and
Tommy, who tripped and smashed his teeth
Against a parking meter and lisps, and
Jessica, whose daddy killed himself and who
Has words but does not use them, and Jan,
Who came from Poland and is still afraid,
He has words too. We all have words.

But the point, we must get back to the point.
We are wasting time, class, the point.

One jay perches on the slightest possible
Branch outside the classroom window.
The jay has no point, no point whatsoever.
And now it has taken itself away from that
Highest point on that highest flammable
Tree. (Look, the smoke comes in the window.
The heat melts the glass. *Smoke*. This is
A word. And, *Death*, even this—this
Pocked and sprawling thing—is a word.)
*Suffer*…a red word that rivals sunset.
*Unto*…a bitter word which is a drawbridge.
*Me*…often used for rhyme, in itself
Green, odd, ageing; green as stagnant water;
Old as guilt; possessing no rhyme at all.
Students, who are of the world, I have watched
You more closely than you would like to think,

Or I. All day you have been growing houses out
Of your shoes; trimmed lawns and fences, mail-
Boxes from your ankles. Bloody beasts with purple
Hands come from your calves. Husbands and wives
Emanate from your loins. Your stomach spews out
Recipes, jobs, resumes, offices, orders, pools
Of chocolate, medicines. Your chest sprouts
Children, nation, grandparents with flags,
Your neck stretches for a faith in things. Your
Mouth, apologies, and curses, and prayers.
Your eyes brighten. They have a private story.
But I see hovering at the small of your back
A kind of angel—that is, if an angel
Could grow old, and not fearing, and be
Grossly independent, and have educational theories.
He looks for employment, he dips down
Into your spine and comes up pouring out
Castles, mansions, châteaux, ponds
Of black elegant swan, water lilies encircling
The row boats white and gently rocking,
A garden party for gnomes and gargoyles,
Maids running everywhere naked on the wet grass,
Governesses fornicating with butlers
Near the table setting of roasted lamb,
Knights at the hoof of dragons,
Twenty-five catapulted marshmallows
Exploding in, smearing the sky....
                              We must get back to
The point: Teaching the Literature
To Children of the World.
                              Take the plastic
Rings from your fingers and turn the ignition,
Signal the passing lane and proceed.

We must get back

The point. How long we have been off.
Oh yes, the jay.

*The Jay has flown away.*

*I want to say I have not aged a day,*
*Children, in years. Not a day.*
*While you lie about, lingering, delighted*
*In the only conceivable world, I*
*Wander halfway—halfway there and*
*Halfway back. Able to tell myself*
*And unable to believe: not a day, not a day,*
*One day I will walk to this door, which*
*Is surely a word, only to find the*
*Door.*

*Which is nothing. Then from a great height there will*

*Fall jays. Bluejays.*                          *Bluejays.*
*Mute radiant bluejays. And, once, I still can recall,*
*I considered everything, how bad things were...*

But there is only one story you must absolutely hear.
Though no one else can tell it to you.
Nor does it make much of a difference,
On the surface of things, I mean.
Monsters will still creep under your bed
When your eye are shut and disappear
The instant you spy them. Dogs will still
Chase you down in the street for no reason.
Your brothers will sometimes have other parents.
I have discarded my notes, but no matter.
Sit in the crotch of the peppermint tree, and look.
Have you ever heard more birds, could you
Imagine a ground that was greener, would the sky
Lift you up spinning were it bluer,

And the flowers, is there any scent softer?
You must remain a few seasons close to the ground.
When birds leave and the sky darkens
And the flowers wither, keep a hold.
Twenty years from now things will be the same.
All you ever wish for unfortunately comes true,
And the birds sympathize with you. It is not
Ever enough, is it? It somehow does not suffice.
You progress on the surface of the earth,
What with the rotation of things, and yet,
You wander everywhere asking untranslatable
Questions. Then it rains, and gently. Birds return.
Tell yourself the only story. Fill in the ending.

I am hurrying through material which
Is not covered in your text, children,
For which you are nonetheless responsible.
But turn now to the unmapped territory,
*There*...which lost its name long ago and
Meet me *there* meeting myself and meet your-
Selves staring blankly at the jade wall where
Wells of coldest water echo often and very
Beautifully. We can approach each other now.
Child, you have grown
So very old.
                    You must be glad.
Children, we have spoken of words enough for today.
Any day you will be tested.
Now we will learn to be silent.

# IN THE PREGNANT GARDEN

Twenty-five days and we'll have zucchini,
In two months more there will be snow pea,
In three months more a child.

The world is too violent to usher in a
Squash, so many generations of
Stony uncultivated fields and plots gone to seed.

Today, though, Sunday between us
Under the sun, the one season for giving
Birth, you pick away at the weeds,

Wander marvelous among the artichokes,
Bitter lettuce, peppers, and California poppies,
Radiant, about to bloom.

# THE STARLIKE EXPRESS

# NEW POEMS

# BEING AT HOME IN YOU

Seasons house us, tongue & groove,
Tongue & groove, ducts & beams.

Love in search of other worlds?
My heart & hands are full in this.

Joist & clamp, mortar & stud,
Roof, frame, floor, tongue & groove.

Sighs desire: this is all that is.
Transferred load, flashing & frame.

Stairs & tile, pitch & stone,
Plumb & charge, tongue & groove.

To fit snug in one world is all
That holds me here in thrall to time.

Flue & wall, window & door,
Insulating, brace, stucco & trim,
Conduit you, tongue & groove.

# ON READING A GREAT POET, NOW GONE

His coyotes scream, scheme for sympathy,
Bridges groan and rust, fields go fallow overnight,
Steamfitters wheeze through the graveyard shift.
The poet is always on the road out of town,
Where it always seems winter in Syracuse,
And where I am, nothing matters, except
Out of Brooklyn, anywhere, backseat overladen
With recollection, stories of the dead.
To get it right is impossible, which is
Why we must leave. To get it right,
To speak with those who have stolen off on
The trip to take alone. It's a long, long way to where
They rest, the dead, and it takes almost no time
At all to arrive. Cap pulled down tight,
Sunglasses fixed, staring straight-faced
Through the windshield into the stormy night.
Alongside nobody, on the winter road out of town.
Someday I just might drive right through the sun, where
Springtime upstate, unpromised, might ever come.

# HEISENBERG, REVISITED

She said, "You're living with uncertainty now."
I knew about *loving* with uncertainty, because—
Come on, who does not? Not to mention *leaving*
With uncertainty and once or twice even *leasing* with
Uncertainty—go on, try renting in a college town.
Blame Heisenberg, baby. I am particle, I am wave.

Everybody knows you can't measure location and
Momentum at the same time but I cannot explain.
And so *between* the moment the application whooshes
Into the aspirational mailbox *and* the crashing career:
Slowly flotillas sink to the bioluminescent ocean floor.
Blame Heisenberg, baby. You are particle, you are wave.

*Between* the moment I come upon, face to face,
A mountain lion—tawny gold, backlit on the sunset trail—
*And* telling park rangers I drummed a pan with a spoon,
Then did the YMCA dance move with uplifted arms:
Seasons flip, from hurricane, huddled in the upstairs dark,
To black diamond run, coruscating alpine slopes.
Blame Heisenberg, baby. They are particles, they are waves.

*Between* the moment children exit, wailing, from a womb,
*And* when they usher into the world wailers of their own:
Haiku, heartbeat, pencil lead shaving, shadow.
Blame Heisenberg, baby. You are particle, you are wave.

*Between* the shared glance locked in across the room
*And* the weekender marathon: a continent crossed,
Lit up by a comet, here, there, now, then, trail of light.
*Between* the brush lifted up before the canvas's blankness
*And* the champagne spillage at the museum installation:
I am fooling nobody. The painting never comes to be,
Unfinishedness is my masterpiece, excuse me while I wait for
The other shoe to drop, the check to clear, the light to go green.
Blame Heisenberg, baby. They are particles, they are waves.

*Between* beginning to write about "living with uncertainty"
*And* living in and with and through uncertainty:
Let's say this is a sunny summer day,
And a baby's being wheeled in a carriage through the park,
And an old man on a bench is feeding pigeons,
Flouting municipal directives, fedora askew
—all of a piece: child, man, pigeon, cubes of bread.
The bruised skies blacken, cloudburst, monsoon.
Umbrellas pop like mushrooms, dogs bounce around drunk,
And everyone flees to the shuttered movie house nearby,
Where they stare into the blank screen a long, long time.

Blame Heisenberg, gorgeous. You are desire,
My particle, and I am nothing if not your wave.

# AND SO, THE NIGHT

Fuck off, I'm late for the colloquy of the owls,
The summer air's still, what's with candles, ooh-la-la?

Boat hulls questionably thump against the dock,
Night blooming jasmine casts off its mauve cape,

Such the homecoming queen. Just like you & me. Wait:
Whose steps echo through the sleepless house?

Question for you in my chair: Were we meant for this world?

Because what's the use counting hours till we halt
Counting hours keeping count of us counting ours?

Wine's lacking, drugs disappoint, how'd we get to this?
I'm going to unmoor a willing boat and find out.

And I will light my way down harborside,
Keeping jittery company with the dead, the not yet.

And so, the night.

# CHURCH UNGOING LATE & SOON

Sunday afternoon once more, thinking about the next world,
Which is very hard to think about any day of the week.
There once was a time for Sunday rituals conceived
Around that afterlife. Only now I conclude that
The next world is not my problem. No, it's yours,
Since you asked for it, being somebody I'd like to be
With when the curtain comes down on this old world.
As worlds go, this one does have its good points
Mixed in with the bad. All of it obvious but
Unsatisfying to contemplate. What if the next world
Is precisely like this one? That would be a disappointment:
The tedious alternatives—cloud portals, translucent
Columns, 24-hour pizza on demand—even if hours don't
Apply up here (just hang with the "up" for now).
Maybe overrun with all your past dogs remembered
And others' dogs, too, only these dogs can talk,
Can tell stories, which we always suspected they could.
And wine's overflowing, raiments overflowing, tresses
Overflowing, all of us gathered in the town square that
Is neither town nor square, and everybody's listening to
Songs they listened to that first time in love and in bed,
And everyone's in love all over again, stupid in love,
Crying and laughing in love, everyone in love,
Nobody lost for now. This, the longest road trip of all time
(despite, again, no road, no time), and we are all
Simply happy to be on the way to wherever it was

We once longed to go. Here's when we cue up
Our most ravishing hallucination, playing out in
Four, five dimensions (who can track? you can't).
And you find your seat at the table in your favorite
Restaurant and order the entire menu,
Why bother to choose, in the next life, right?
And when the check comes, you're sated and hungry both,
And there's no bill to pay anymore. But wait, is that God
In the kitchen in his filthy apron, sautéing up a storm?
Maybe, and you find yourself outside beneath a cloud
Of arrested cherry blossom. You knew all along you knew nothing,
The best part of being in the next world is to realize
Nowhere's left to go anywhere but here,
Right now, and the world you left behind is
The world that is always leaving behind you.

# ON LOSING FRIENDSHIP AT AN ADVANCED AGE

Jumped in the car that day and off we were,
Just as we always did and not quite like before.
A fine day it was, like one of those daydreams
Of flight and fecklessness. Let's stop, I thought,
For lunch. Name one thing unimproved by sandwiches.
The waiter recited the endless list of specials
And I felt despair all over again, at least a new despair.
You know what we really need, you said.
*Psilocybin.* Maybe later, I said, we need time
To slow down. Exactly, you said, *psilocybin.*
Next, then, somehow we were at the shore,
Waves crashing upon the naked throng
Of merrymakers. Is any misery not magnified
By showing up among merrymakers? Exactly,
You said again, contra-contra-indicating psilocybin.
Do not say *psilocybin* ever again, I said.
Let's go, we'll be late for the opera.
But I am always late for the opera,
Optimal way to miss the Ride of the Valkyries.
But never Puccini, how can you not love Puccini?
We should have had lunch, only now it's too late.
There's no going back, though the specials sounded good.
You don't know the first thing about reality, you barked,
The specials are what you never should order,
It's fish they have to use before it turns bad,
Meat sauce-slathered to disguise discontent.

I had to concede you were a citizen of unreality,
And I'm at best a tourist. The day's turned out a bust.
No sea, no naked celebrators, no opera, no lunch.
What's left for us to withstand? We should just drive,
I said, like we used to, meandering along,
Finding our way to finding our way back home.
When we were friends, remember then?
I sure do recall, that's when we were both alive.
But we'll always return to the sea. Look to
The birds overhead, behold the cresting waves,
It's enough to want to take a long, long drive
With you again. Why don't you take the wheel,
I said. No response, which was to be expected
Insofar as it was just me, on the way from
Wherever we once used to be, a ragtag cortege
In disarray. Everything once remembered, you would
Have said, feels like dying. Except for death,
Don't forget, I said, which feels like nothing but
The last mad marvel of the squandered moment,
The unmasking of us all as night falls. The end.

# TRAUMA, SOME USES OF

What a trestle bridge upcountry is for, middle of the night.
What being there alone is for, river current rippling below,
Water mirroring the moon's fat shivery face.
This is why you're here.
                         Then the sky splits apart,
A blue-black taut canvas rips in two, which you almost can hear.
The drop from this height a thing to consider, a boat to wish for
Docked on the near side of the shore. Which is
When through the jagged opening looms another seldomed sky
Along with another brighter moon. Broken parts of you
Fall along the tracks, too late for a note to write, born too late,
As the wolves lope across the bridge, come to save you
From taking refuge in the beyond within yourself.

# WRITE WHAT YOU KNOW

*To DY*

Write what I *know*? All right, that won't take too long,
Leaving all the time in the world for pickle ball and TV.
Maybe I'll step right up to bat and take my hacks.
Speaking of which, I know what my walk-up-to-the-plate
Music is, if I were a pro baseball player, which I am
In my bustling fantasy life. That music would be
Beethoven's Fifth Symphony, which is long enough
To postpone indefinitely seeing blow past me strike three.
Many things I *used* to know, and have diplomas for proof.
Now, I do know I have never once used the word *archipelago*
In anything I have ever written or tried to write, which,
When you think about it, is an absurd distinction.
Makes me contemplate all the words waiting still
To be abused, exploited, deracinated, or shagged by yours truly,
Which brings up the sheer tonnage of words untouched by me.
This in itself may be the perfect summation of a failed life,
Depending on how you think about summations and failures
And life and the vanity project called writing what you know.
But *archipelago* is a throaty, mouthy, tongue-curl full lip lock
Of a word, so you'd think there'd been call for it sometime,
In love with islands and deep waters as you claim to be,
Said I, talking to myself addressed as *you* as I am wont to do.
I'd understand better write *how* you know, even *when*
You know, or *if* you know, and when it comes to my meager
Career accomplishments the dreaded *who* you know.

In that vein, find attached my c.v. for your light entertainment.
As for *my* entertainment, take the subject of the unconscious.
Dreaming is implicated there, and dreaming is fabulous
Even if most dreams are—let's be honest—kind of boring.

But take last night, the dream in which you appeared,
First time since you died. You're holding the empty picture frame
And standing inside the vacated space, as you liked to do,
And you're here to tell me you are glad, glad we had the chance
To fix what was broken between us—while we're both alive,
Although one of us famously was not technically alive.
Seems like an important distinction, although not in my dream.
It was good to see you, my onetime former and future friend,
Even though you weren't there because maybe you never were
Or always would be, or we never were, given the fact you were dead
Though not to me, come on, look, you were there in the dream
Making peace between us, something I know for the first time forever,
And see? I have written it, crossing the archipelago of time,
Islands in the stream, so it must be true. I am on the last pontoon,
Alongside you.

# MY NEW SCHOOL OF POETRY

The Zen monk's chanting drifted unto the trees,
Quasi-good news for morning meditation.
That'll tell you what kind of day it was.
Then I couldn't decide what sort of electric car
To buy, having no money, insofar as they were all
Priced out of my budget, which I also didn't have.
Instead I would found my own school of poets.
Like the New York, the Black Mountain, hell,
Like Imagists, Metaphysicals, the Romantics,
The Modernists, the Confessionals, the Beats.
I had the perfect brand, too. We would be the
*Post-Contemporary School.* (Yeah, good question,
I don't know what it means either!)
It just occurred in a flash! Meta, or what, man?
When the school meets—if we meet—we would have
No agenda (so Beta, right?). No flagship
Journal to publish our superstar emerging types
Alongside heavy hitters whose acolytes write blurbs.
We would simply *be*...post-contemporary poets.
We would read each other's work by moonlight, or
All the computer monitor pixels would pixilate about.
Will we have a manifesto? Of course not, and why?
Because we are post-contemporary poets, is why.
No application process, no MFA required,
Everyone's eligible, no one's admission denied.
But just be sure not to show up empty-handed at

Our soon-to-be-famous soirées—say we ever have some
Of those. Of course, somebody will want to cook up
Websites or antisocial media, and that's okay, *because*?
Because yes, we are post-contemporary poets is why.
We will have no marching orders, no guru, no boss.
I don't care if you are the next Kenneth Koch or
Thomas Chatterton, the boy genius who shut up
Wordsworth and Coleridge, back in the day of
Tricorner hats, muskets, and loving your sibling
A tad too inappropriately, but then he died.
Dying is all right, though, you can still qualify for the school.
But I digress. (And that's okay, too, need I explain why?)
One day, just you wait, a million poets will clamber onboard
The post-contemporary express, there's room!
Don't count on a destination for this school of poets.
Don't come here for "advice for writers," or
How to get an agent (you're funny), or workouts, or recipes.
You'll be disappointed, which, come to think of it,
Is on brand for us, branded poets bereft of brand.
But enough, I see I've gone on too long. (Which is…
You know.) Stop being the poet on the lookout for
The next Emily the D or Ezra the P (without the anti-Sem-
Itism) or Frank O the H, or Silvia the P. Our poems
Are drafty, foundationless houses minus roofs and doors,
Open to the sky (watch your head, Walt the W).
Stay focused, if you wish. But if you can't, all right.
We're all just here, waiting for you to break into song,
If song, that is, is your thing, and who's to deny you?
Nobody! This is our school in a nutshell.
Yours and mine. Look in your heart, and you know, go
Post-contemp. There's precisely everything else to lose.

# REPORT FROM COUPLES' COUNSELING

It's not easy being me.
No, it's easier being you
Whoever you are,
Busily not being me all
The livelong day. Sit down
Right there and tell me
Your story, leave nothing out.
The ride to the shore,
The sea lion carcass beached,
The sacristy of the dunes,
The seaweed in your hair
When your body surfaced
A hundred years before
You ever became you.
Only now I recall who I once was,
Before I became you, such
A burden, remembering anything,
The wind that picked up on the street
That time, and you laughed to lose
Your hat, tumbling along till
It disappeared in the night,
The way you also did then,
And the way I am now
Without you, being me, being you,
Missing that hat you said
You wore for who I once was to you.

# GIRL, 12, IN TRANSITION

You texted me: "You have a grandson now."
How shadowy is that word *have*.
Can I have for long water cupped in my hand?
Can I have memory of you from the before?
I also require one more lifetime to digest *now*.
But let's stipulate this is not about me,
Yet who's the me stipulating as to the you?
Thank you for writing, the you you were in
Transition to the you you are unbeknownst.
Everything, everyone in a whirl of transition,
No points fixed, like the stars that only appear
To be fixed against the black scrim that stretches
Across the sky. Because you always were the light,
Which will never dim, which will never blink,
Would always be who, the who you mean to be.

# DOMINION OF DESIRE

Another epoch, continent, universe, and
I might have been king or even queen.
The same might be said of you, though
You would have been better at the job,
Which is clearly no job at all. Me, I'd
Wander, sable-clad, and crown around,
Decree to no purpose, manically deem
Drawbridges to lift where they do not exist,
Demand vats of finest wine, though wine
Is not for me (just ask my endocrinologist—
Only if you dare), order cavalries to mount
For mock battle, knight all my high school pals.
Because listen: Falling in love means you feel
Like royalty. Your body mine, one sovereign domain.
It's awkward to lay claim, but desire is not
A democracy or a republic, has no parliament—
Is no oligarchy or kleptocracy, of course not.
But our bed would be sumptuous by fiat.
And our nights would be infinite, our days warm, sunlit.
See, this sort of desire makes us crazed and drunk
With sway over time and mortality, over which
Otherwise we have no dominion until, that is,
Your embrace, the whole world whirling 'round you.

# A FRIEND TELLS ME HE HAS DEMENTIA

Far beyond any trail I ever hiked,
Where you could not hear the crash of the sea,
Or catch the gleam of distant city lights below,
I come upon a cabin abandoned.
Busted windows, battered door, rusted pot belly stove.
Scat, rat droppings pattern the warped wood floor,
Pine table overturned, tipped-over wicker chair.
I've never prayed but I'm not sure I wanted to.
If God needed my attention, he failed to qualify.
The monks who taught me in school would say
I had it backwards, and they are doubtless correct.
Yet tell me why this space felt sacred,
Though I think I already know. Abandonment is
Spiritual practice, and whoever once lived here
Has left this life behind. For which
I cannot find fault. One day here, next day,
Not, what else is there to say anymore?
Whoever lived here has renounced all claim.
We stock our life's shelves with remembrance
Only to be someday forgot. Time to walk off
Away from all we know, or believed we did.
I thought about where I had been going
And why I should now turn back. To find
In the woods this desolated chapel
Is enough to bring me down to my knees.
I want to remember my friend as he was and will be.

So I keep thinking, standing in this cabin,
He'll walk back in and tell me what he's found
In the world uncontained by these four walls.
Listen, he'd say. He meant to the birds.
He was right, it was an old song, made new again.
I'll hold on to this song for him, in case
He needs to recollect.

# ON THE BRIEF HISTORY OF MY AUTHOR PHOTOS

That was me back then, looking askance like a champ
At nothing in particular, *askance* being a vocation
Of mine. On balance, let me say I'm unbalanced.
Then there's this one: buzz cut, black glasses, trimmed beard,
Like I'm auditioning for an off-off-Broadway play,
Like for a role I never will in a million years get.
That book did not do very well, wonder why.
Oh and here's one of me in front of a precarious
Mountain of books about to avalanche.
I look like I don't know how I got there,
And it's true, that's not even my house.
My last book: my face creased, deckle-
Edged like a fine print first edition, I wish.
I forgot this other one, where I am staring off
Into the distance, not looking at you, dear
Putative reader or book-buyer as if I'm thinking,
Buzz off, gentle soul, why don't you already?
There's also this one: cannot recall who convinced
Me to fold my arms like that. An OG look
But of course I achieve the opposite effect.
Oh, right, the ex's idea. Convenient to blame
The ex. Maybe I deserved eventual dismissal
For ironically dedicating the book to somebody else,
Soon to be relegated to ex-ex-status forthwith.
One author photo I wish had been shot:
Me in the Piazza Navona or the Tuileries

Or Central Park, with a flock of hovering birds
Over my head, a few perched on my shoulders.
I truly regret that other one in the cowboy hat—
What was I thinking? But not the shot at
The ranch, stroking the palomino's mane,
Her gaze more profound than any sentence of mine.
Looking at these photos, I see I have ruined
Everything. I posed and I posed and I posed,
To what end? All of them nakedly pleading:
Trust me, want me, reach out to me.
I am nothing but a book for you to open
Some lonely afternoon or sleepless night,
Which is when I wrote it, for you, or so
I want you to believe. Take me into your arms
Awhile and I will never leave you again.
I am all yours if you want, and you are mine
To take into bed, lighting a candle
Left on the winter windowsill. Careful now,
Whoever you are, candles can be treacherous, too.

# BRIEF ADVENTURES IN DATING

See the birds rise up and riot midair above the field?
No, beyond that farther tree line, yes, right there.
You can hear if you want the distant strains of
Music, the melody of late autumn afternoon,
A vertiginous gust of golden leaves rustling adrift.
We might have traveled there sometime, to where
Lovers gather on the gleaming lakefront, where
Bathers joust, boats bob in the wind-shifting current.
Isn't it amazing we once used to be here with others?
I speak rhetorically, maybe theoretically, though you know
The theory of our acquaintance is as incontrovertible
As prismatic sunspots that stipple your face blue-green,
Eyes dilating as time together comes to a lenient close.

# SELECTIONS FROM THE RECENTLY UNCOVERED
# UNDATED UNPAGINATED JOURNALS OF

Burn this now just burn this now

*

I yearn exclusively for whatever's hazardous to
Myself. It displeases me no end to be one with
The human species, about whom I've heard
Distant and unverified reports of war
And love brutally breaking out.
The food at this hotel is wretched. What's
So tough about a taco, an omelet, an oyster shucked?

*

You're still reading you monster burn this now.
These scribbled notations are merely the chemtrails
Beclouding your self-satisfied horizons. (Nice one, tough guy.)

*

News of the big fat prize being given me came as
A shock, as in, what took them so fucking long?
Explaining my banishment to this horrible hotel.
First sentence in my obit will reference its bestowal
And my job from now on is to forestall that development.
I need to work on my acceptance remarks:
"I would like to thank M for writing my book."

*

I do love M but it is L I crave.
I should be less cruel to M, but they make me
(Wait what)

*

The earthquake shook me out of bed just then.
Then the aftershocker temblor. Nothing can
Kill me anymore, I am invincible. I claim that
Minibar for My Majesty, give up your veiled treasures.
But M! Listen to me, M! why don't you come
To my house anymore? True, I'm in a vile
Hotel tonight, but that is beside the point,
Which is also true about me in general.
I may just burn down your house so you have
Nowhere else to turn, my go-to seduction ploy,
A technique which is suddenly (seduction, that is) such
A bad thing yeah right, not that I have much
Of a case to make, having lost track of the meds.
(I call this riff the resurrection blues.)
*

Swimming is overrated. (Oh yes, see? I take my chances
Spouting unpopular opinions, which is what artists—
And cranks like me—are required to do.)
Overrated, except for when you're in the deep end
And not swimming would be considered most postmodern.
I reflected on the swimming subject as I skinny-dipped
In the indoor pool tonight, and gave myself a medal for
Reaching the other side alive, where the loyal bottle
Awaited to be killed forthwith. After one more lap.
*

Hey, *pets*? Why does everybody have pets these days?
Now, there's nothing wrong with animals. I could go
And live with animals—quoting a poet I once loved.
But pets? That's different. Yes, they are pets, but only
Because we surgically remove the animal from them.
*

Barolo, the uber-pricey vino of the Italians?
Umm, no thanks. Tastes like old socks.

Not that I can actually, you know, confirm
From first-foot experience. Also overrated—
Much as I am, tomorrow prize bash notwithstanding—
Psychotherapists. As lovers, I mean, overrated.
Psychotherapy is just fine, all those made-up stories.
I can testify to the truthfulness of my view,
And I did my part entertaining, teaching my shrinks.
I am at a party, and therapists are drawn to me
Metal shavings to the anvil—an image I will need
To rethink if I ever reread this journal,
And which you should stop looking at right now.
The therapist strikes up a conversation, I can tell
They need help and then there's me in bed with them.
Afterwards, beforewards too, and talk talk talk
Lots of talking. Not much to narrate about
The interim between after and before,
When you are always on my mind, M.
Another topic shrinks like to undress.

                    *

This eminent philosopher writes that boredom is both
A feeling and the absence thereunto of feeling. As proof,
Of her insouciance and perspicacity and
Other SAT words, I offer up the previous sentence
As well as this whole journal, which I notice—
Well, I'm not noticing anything anymore—which
I gather you are still besmirching if not besmooching with your
Consciousness, such as it is, or was. Is the SAT
Still a thing in the world? I've thrown out my new book,
The whole thing. Not literally, you cannot throw
Out anything anymore on account of technologies
In which I am nonfluent. Feeling and absence both, Amen.

                    *

A professor invited me into their college classroom,
Guest reading or lecture or something. I showed up
In a clean jacket and shirt, with actual books in tow.
That was the day my agent called with news,
A nice fat option taken out, some streaming channel,
So I was full of myself, though no more than usual.
Everybody in the room looked to be twelve,
It was frightening. I shouldn't be allowed to be
Around children (just ask my own, if they will speak
To you). At the appropriate time I began to read.
At the inappropriate time, half the class fled the room.
I knew there was pain and suffering adduced in my prose,
If you would be so kind as to call my stuff that.
You know what I did. I followed them out.
I'm not safe enough to be around myself.

*

Some of my favorite hallucinations involve B.
(Is that you, B, reading this? I hereby grant provisional access.)
Sure, why don't I just write out B's name, it's my journal,
My rules apply. Maybe B would be aroused, flattered,
Amused, exonerated. There was a chance, you know.
Maybe I even exist in B's mind, too. All right, long shot.
But in my imagination B is my slinky monkey,
Being neither slinked nor monked in reality.
This hallucination also involves my famous clafoutis,
One with sweet pitted cherries. Suck on that, food critics.
If my fans only knew how weird I was (but they do),
How fluid (in my mind at least) were B's boundaries
And B's bank accounts. Ah, that's the theme for my acceptance!

*

The key to making a perfect omelet is—a riddle
To me. Sure, you have room temp eggs (you know that, M).
Sweet Irish or French butter. I hear of devotees of

288

Admixing crème fraiche to the froth of whipped eggs.
Call me a convert. Heat is important, but not too high,
Don't be impatient. The key to eating a great omelet is
L finally making me a great omelet, tomatoes, chives,
Grated gruyère. Remembering L's omelet, I'm in love
Again for the first time. Just like with M.

*

The problem with the competitive game of tennis is:
I am terrible at it. Plus, the shorts, look what time has wrought.

*

Everything changes, everything ends.
Read that in a smarter-than-expected self-help book
B threw at me stomping out the door for good,
It was claimed. It made me remember M
And then, sigh, L, and how everything changed,
Everything ended. L stole my other journal,
The one nobody will never find, good luck,
Learning the distressing-to-L truth about M and about B.
Next thing I knew, I was all alone again.
There are worse things than being alone.
None of which I can tonight recall.
L did plead: get help, you really need help,
Sometime we all need help. I quoted B's book:
How everything changes, everything ends.
You're a very sad case, L said, L not being
L's initial.

*

Longtime readers of moi know I never desecrate
The page with exclamation points too busy defiling them
With my prose rants but that got me to thinking
Always dangerous the thinking got me to thinking
About losing all forms of punctuation which
Was a liberation and I started to discard the rest

Like the niggling comma the arch semicolon
The EM dash whatever the fuck EM means oh
It was glorious to feel so free again aching one day
To reach the precipice of meaningfulness
Bereft of a parachute under which to drop down from the heights .
*

You swore you would burn this you promised me so
*

Oh L Oh M Oh B all of you versions of myself
But you L, I loved best of all good night sweet dreams

# ONCE I WAS A MAN WHO KNEW BLISS

Bliss's first name was Frank. Officially, Franklin.
But Frank Bliss, to be candid, was nothing of the sort.
A sniveler and a snitch, all through school. Fine,
Sure, we were close, in a distant kind of way,
As you would be with someone who never paid
You back the lunch money he owed. I think you get
Saddled with a name like Franklin, it's hard
To pay off your debts, or that's what strikes me.
And yes, I did strike *him* once or twice in
His prominent nose, prominent for being packed
With drugs, which he peddled around the yard.
You would understand why I stole his drugs
One time, which he deserved, Franklin that he was.
Next day he came to school with a tire iron,
A serious tool, though ill-suited for taking final exams,
Which he famously failed. Poor guy, old Frankie Bliss,
Who had lots more money than I had or that
He could ever use, especially after I ripped him off.
If you ask me, we have all known some Bliss
When we were younger. Which reminds me of
The poem we were forced to memorize in class.
*Whenever Richard Cory went downtown we people*
*On the pavement looked at him* and so on. Edward
Arlington Robinson. I myself can't use a middle name
But Frank could, especially if he ends up like the punk
Cory in the poem we took to heart. Spoiler alert: Not

So good. Let that be a lesson to Frank. Anyway,
Frankie Bliss, in order to have a poem with his name,
Should be Franklin *Cumberland* Bliss. Has a ring.
The whole thing makes me feel relieved Teachers
Of America probably no longer assign "Richard Cory"
By E. A. Robinson. Maybe the only good development
To relate on the status of our great national experiment
Known as the United States of America. Our Great
National Experiment smells like one that went wrong,
Chem class: Rotten eggs. Old Frankie Bliss: Wonder what
Happened to the guy. If our paths should cross outside
A poem's confines, I'll make it up to him, poor son of a bitch.
And one day, maybe at our next reunion,
I'll return to him freshly stained his school sweatshirt.
Least I could do for a lying pal of mine, clean favored
And, like the old poet says, imperially slim.

# WONDERS NEVER CEASING

Once I was beloved. And no, I don't believe it, either.
"Where do you get your ideas?" they all asked.
"Who does your hair?" Seemed like I'd never pay
A bar tab again. In despair, I started shaving my legs.
I don't think this *beloved* part had anything to do with
My winning the Powerball Lottery. Man, five bucks:
Not a lot to pay for a dream come true. In no time,
Strangers dedicated rock and roll memoirs to me,
Pleaded with me to be godparent to
Their precious offspring, they took out my recycling,
Kept me company on the DMV registration line,
Baked me Boston cream pies, shared their Ecstasy.
I should have started playing the Lottery before,
After she left me, and he left me, and the pink-
Handle razors rusted out on the side of the tub,
A reporter knocked on my door—only visitor
To my new digs with the turrets and the gated
Perimeter.
    "How'd you get inside," I asked,
Polite as any mega-zillionaire you ever met.
"I'm Cassandra," she said. "Has wealth changed you?"
Listen, I still pull on my Chanel pants one leg
At a time. Then I opened a '47 Lafite to shut
Her up. I could have said no, I could have said
Yes, I could have said get out of my face.
But money confers privileges my previous

Teaching assistant stipend did not. So I took
Cassandra for a spin around the estate
In my new jade Bentley—well, I asked her to drive.
"Money is a kind of poetry," she said. "Wallace
Friggin Stevens," I said, "great poet not as rich
As me."

      "I could fall for you," she said.

                             "May I call you
Cassie?"

      "Whatever, but do you miss your former life?"
"You mean like buying bus passes, baking tuna
Casseroles, shopping at Costco?" I predicted
Where she was going, like a Cassandra. I buzzed
Security to hustle her out pronto, because I might
Fall for Cassie, too. Is there such a thing as former lives?
It moved me to wondering if I was destined to be briefly
Beautiful and if I should shave my legs ever again.

# AT THE SITE OF MY NEW BURIAL PLOT

*We Poets in our youth begin in gladness;*
*But thereof come in the end despondency and madness.*
—Wordsworth, "Resolution and Independence"

Leech-gatherers once were preferred care
And 19th-century Romantic poetry providers.
It's uncommon these days to run into them
On crosstown subway lines, but you seek for leeches
In marsh and bog so the A train's worth a shot.
Nearest I get to bloodletting in my ville
Is the corner dive called The Last Roundup Saloon.
That's where Leech-Gather Conventioneers
Congregate, because the Roundup sucks—
Too easy, but true. I myself spend more time
With shamans, witch doctors, life coaches, shrinks,
With the occasional unibrowed oncologist thrown in.
About the Last Roundup: who knew loneliness
Could be so loud, besides everybody assembled
At Our Lady of Perpetual Leech Gather Cemetery?
A bucolic place thus far unfrequented by 19th-century
Romantic poets where I'm one day supposed
To finally rest my weary, brittle, decalcifying bones.
At least there's a nice stone bench and a sapling that
Promises serious shade for my future ambivalence.
Time was—and it was, it truly *was*—time was,
Barbershops were prime bloodletting sites, a noble
Pursuit in the cause of Therapeutic Phlebotomy,

A perfect name for a saloon in which I'd gladly invest.
Hence the candy stripe, red and white pole
Advertising services: trim, shave, slice, and cut.
I promise not to bring up how hair does not grow
Beneath the earth inside one's steely bier—which
Reminds me: IPA at the Roundup is the lure
For college kids crossing the choppy moat drawbridge,
Flags fluttering, screen door flapping from the twister's
Approach. Later they projectile vomit on the street,
Who can blame them, college being what it is
And the Last Roundup. My restless roundup
Will be Our Lady of Unquenchable Leeches.
Come here, little boys, girls, and bloodletters,
I have my MRIs, and someday you'll have yours.
Who wouldn't be caught dead at closing time,
Who'll belly up at the Roundup for last call?

# WELCOME TO YOUR PODCAST

Today 's theme: *The Motorcycle Lifestyle*, but mainly
On your show you lament your lost *joie de vivre*.
Everybody's lamenting something on your podcast.
You need to call yourself out—who was it who stole
Your will to survive? Your meditative lurch?
Today you talk about a book everybody should
Take into their bosom, was how you phrased it. You're
So old school: You speak the word "bosom." It isn't so bad.
You kind of like it. Bosom. Bosom. Bosom. Bosom.
*Bosom* some more. Namaste, motherfucker. You can't
Say that, either. You wax serious all of a sudden—
Don't get me started on "wax." Fact is, lots of kids
Were shot today again in a school. Screw the minute of
Silence. You suggest several hours of screaming rage.
Not that that does anybody any good, least of all
The kids who bled out.
                          With time to fill
You propose Five Tips to Endure the Insanity.
Four Recipes for a Loser Dinner Party. Three Tunes
For Crashing the High School Reunion. Two New Names
For Misery in the Afternoon, but they are the same
Names they've always been. Welcome to your podcast.
You forget? Today's show's all about motorcycles,
Which it will be when you hop on your hog Harley
And blow town, head to the Staples Center
And your courtside seats for another big game.

You and your loss: soulmates. Your upcoming podcast
Should be all about me, not that you know it or me,
Which is why I'm obsessed with our podcast.
You ask such badass probing questions
You almost wish you had time to hear answers.
All of us out here feel the same same as you
And I'll take my answer off the air.

# SAY SOMETHING

Say something say anything say nothing.
This matters but I don't know how or why.
Then again, not knowing is my signature,
That and my spaghetti carbonara and risotto
Milanese and tiramisu. Cook something
Cook anything, cook nothing. Here it is
California, September, my, what a glorious
Drought we're having. Still, I feel guilty
Enjoying the sunshine on my face
All the while distraught over no rain no snow
Say something say anything don't say
Nothing. On the job-front you should
Hire me you should hire somebody,
Anybody that is not not me. Not that
I would make a difference and drought
Will persist, the planet being on its last legs.
A Northern Flicker hammers its head
Against the oak tree outside my window.
He's out of season, we are all out of
Season now, these days there is the absence
Of seasons except for the season of drought
And the positions no one will hire me for.
I'm not really qualified for those jobs
But neither are you when you consider
So much work left undone not to mention
The supply chain being broken. Me, I am one

With that fractured supply chain. If I ever mend it
I will heal in new places still broken
And the drought ravages the earth
And everything else beside the drought.
In the beginning there was talk of
The beginning as if it could be marked
On a map a graph resembling a supine
Body poolside with Margarita and chips,
A flowchart, an ancient text recovered
In the Mojave in the thousand-year drought.
Trick is, beginning implied the opposite,
Which is not ending but beginning and
Beginning all over again. That's why
Say something say anything don't say nothing.

# DIAGNOSIS

To the top of the snowy mountain they led me,
The secret place where the cold, cold water flowed.
*Drink your fill*, the diagnosticians said. It was good,
And they were scary and required my approval
Or I needed theirs, it was not easy to tell which.
*Let us know when you begin to hear music,*
But that was just the thing. I could not get
The music to stop. Honestly, it proved company,
The hitchhiker in my head you have to pick up
Even if you're not going their way, which is what
Music's all about, nobody's going the same way.
*Watch the pulsing blue light, keep your head still.*
That blue, the most haunting blue I'd ever seen,
A blue so ecstatic, it was enough to make me
Revisit the whole God question. *Tell us the dream
Again you dreamt.* I started to, then they stopped me—
*Not the flying monkeys one again*, they said.
Hey, I possess my own dream, I said. *Ah, that's
Where you are wrong. That's our dream first.*
Enough of this crap, I said. Give it to me straight, doc.
*You're impatient. That's it, that's the diagnosis?*
*We have a theory. Our theory is you're lying.*
Of course, I am lying, but what is the diagnosis
For that? *We have different pharmaceuticals to try.*
Great, I said, let's hope they make you feel better.
*Tell us, Reginald, how long have you lived off the grid.*

I was no Reginald, everybody knew that.
I did not see a way to correct them, they were
Looking more disappointed than ever. So I let
Them insert my body inside one after another
Massive machine of measurement. Afterward,
They hummed like freeway traffic as they scanned
Pixilated charts and graphs. A harpsichord concerto
Kicked up between my ears. This would keep me busy
A while, harpsichord concertos being what they are.
*How about this?* How about what, you fiends?
*Does this hurt?* Fuck, it hurts, you put a clamp
On my head. *Excellent, we're getting somewhere.*
Where's that, I begged. *Hang on—how about this?*
*Can you describe how you feel?* That's easy, psychopaths,
The scalpel hurts, being a scalpel and that's my wrist.
*Great progress, Reginald, you've been such a good patient.*
*Let's try this. Family history. Did you have parents?*
*Were you ever born? Did you once live in a castle?*
Yes to all of the above, I lied, but I'm now going to leave.
*Ah, the pills are kicking in, right on schedule.*
Then like that we were back on the mountain top.
The water tasted better than—it's hard to explain—
Better than water, which is I think impossible, though
True. So this was my diagnosis. My condition incurable.
I was terminal, terminally me. *If there was nothing wrong*
*With you, Reginald, something would be wrong with you.*
Progress at last, I told them, hand me the scalpel.

# IT HAS COME TO MY ATTENTION

A little too late it has come to my attention that
I am wearing the wrong shoes for this hike
Into the mountains. It's also come to my attention
That step by step the road's getting steep.
And it has come to my attention I did not pack
Bear spray and that I'm traveling solo not by choice.
Because it's come to my attention you abandoned me
In the parking lot below, having had "enough of me
For the hundredth time!" It has come to my attention
You have a point. Even so, that doesn't obviate
The fact it's getting colder and colder as sun sets,
As sun is wont to do, as our connection is also
Wont to do. Once upon a time it came to my attention
That I have an attention deficit disorder, which
Diagnosis I cannot recall when I need it most,
Like when wide awake, or here walking on mountains
In the altogether wrong shoes. Ones I'm wearing are
Stylish and perfect for many an occasion (lecture hall,
Symphony, date night, trattoria), only not
For a walk into mountains, night coming on,
The right shoes being in your trunk when you sped off.
Well, I'm glad I packed up the water bottle—
Which it has come to my attention I have not.
That's the moment when it comes to my attention
I'm being tracked by a bear, an unwelcome
Development, given my bear spray-exempt status.

Then it comes to my attention—no bear at all,
But maybe a mountain lion (I am on a mountain,
After all). But no, it was you, there with water
And with my hiking boots and permission
To come back to where I belong, which is
Clearly not here, alone in the mountainous brush.
It has come to my attention that I wish always
To not find myself where I find myself but
Instead, to be loping through a field that thrums
With honeybees, two threatened species in tandem,
In a sea of nasturtiums, bright puckering lips
That make me want to kiss you for finding me
All over again and bringing up the right shoes,
Which has come to my attention, but mainly you.

# THE ALEATORY SHUFFLE

(Go on, I'll wait, go look the word up.)
OK, we good? Cool, from the Latin for "dice."
Throwing dice, that's a thing. You can be trouble
When you try, you know that? If I may
Get to my point, which is not aleatory at all,
This is my report on the search for
Paradise. Yeah, clunky pun spread-eagled there,
Pair-a-dice. Sorry I mentioned. But
We knew from the jump paradise was a long shot.
Still we took all the drugs, read all the books,
Met with masters on mountain tops, camped out,
Burning Man, converted to numerous faiths,
Slept with them all, travelled faraway lands,
Merged across all the known spectrums
And then some, and fell in love again and again,
One soulmate candidate after another, and...
To what end? *That's* the end, paradise. I did learn
Paradise was no sort of place to settle down,
Just an oasis on the way to where dice are thrown
Until against all the odds they roll your way.

# DO YOU SEE I AM A NEW PERSON?

When I slipped into a gossamer black silk shift for you,
You heard the hovering wings of a hummingbird.
Things happen when you're lost, adrift at metaphorical sea,
But okay, one thing. It was sunrise and the dinghy
Was all that kept me between the devil and the deep blue sea.
So yeah, get this, an angel. The Angel Michael, though
I think properly he's an archangel. But he did not
Stand on ceremony with me. He had brought me a breakfast
Burrito and a cup of coffee and—a pineapple!
You never count on a pineapple's arrival on the open
Unmetaphorical sea, do you? It smelled like my childhood
And he sliced it into golden wheels of sweetness.
Thus it was that this very minute I was convinced:
A) I was in mortal peril, or B) I was already dead though
In which case, how'd I get on some dinghy in the first place?,
Or C) I might have become a new person.
"Mike—you okay I call you Mike? Okay, good, thanks,
You're an angel, man." (Which I told you before he was.)
"I have a burning question. Where'd you get the pineapple?"
Because as a miserable child I used to love pineapple,
It was one of the few things that made me glad
Even if it triggered certain food-related issues I'll spare you—
Which along with God made me glad. I was now pretty sure
God was for real again, because look out! angel alert!
One out here on the open sea armed with a beautiful burrito.
Naturally, the question still ached, as in how did I get

On this dinghy anyway, far from land on the open sea?
You could tell Mike was just itching to pounce.
"Hey, you've long been at sea and just never knew it,
Girlfriend." So I was in one big fat metaphor come to life?
*Lost. At sea. Adrift.* Come on. Not cool, God, thought I,
But did not say, the essence of a moot point, being that
God being God knew all along what I was thinking
And what I was not, and since he followed the bouncing ball,
Far be it from me to pick a fight, given the precarity of
The situation. "Is this burrito for really real?"
Mike shook his angelic head, luxurious tresses agleam,
Clearly pitying me for doubting the ontology of
A burrito, which was obvious to the swooping pelican
That then snatched it from my hand. Forgive me, but
I began wondering if life itself is a metaphor, and if so,
For what? It could make a difference, one way or the other,
I suppose.

       Long story short: this whole thing may explain how
I got here at this family dinner table, speculating as to
Whose family this may be, and if someday it could be
Mine, which is when I asked if you could tell I had become
A new person. "I hope you can," I said, "and will tell me
All about it." It's not easy becoming a new person, I bet,
It's a tall order. Someday maybe I should give it a shot.

# THE EMPTINESS

I'm big with the everywhere emptiness, tra la.
When I see birches stripped bare, spectral white,
I recognize my kindred sort of emptiness. Standing
Room only emptiness, it's command performance
Emptiness, a baker's dozen and a prix fixe
Emptiness to ontologically gorge myself upon.
You'd think by now I'd had my fill of
Such ordinary fare at my age, but no,
I'm still getting acquainted with the emptiness.
I cannot say deny the emptiness, because
Even should I say yes, emptiness is all no,
Which is a kind of postprandial fullness, too.
Plus, I've got by heart the musical score,
Hummable, playable, toe-tappingly my own.
Which gets to the main point of this
Emptiness, how it's mine and mine alone,
All I was and all I am subsumed.
Inside of it, the winds blow, trees shiver,
Caverns gleaming, flooding into the estuary,
Sacrificial in its limpidness, its overfullness
That is the emptiness of emptiness of emptiness.
If I were to say to myself, I'm all done now,
What is the point, my emptiness would concur,
Being nothing but an agreeable sort
And nothing at all. It wants nothing, needs
Nothing, pleads nothing but for itself to go on,

Being empty, and on it goes, as if
The emptiness were all that remained,
And should those birches leaf out this spring
Emptiness every time will have a last wintry word.

# HANK VISITS ME FROM THE AFTERLIFE

He's on a rant, which is so, so Hank,
And he's speaking through me.
"And another thing," he goes,
"And the horse you rode in on."
And all I got left is, I'm sorry, man.

Such a night surrounds.
A darkness deeper than mere night
Is everywhere, impinging.
Did you have to pick my birthday
To die on? And he goes,
"Sorry to inconvenience you."

Lives can go very wrong,
Exhibit A, Exhibit Never Mind,
Nothing to prove, nothing to show
For it, once upon a time friends.

Your best poem had in the title
"Constantinople," which I cannot find.
So many things I cannot find anymore,
Like reasons, like decisions, like
Misunderstandings between us.

"The night she died," he said to me,
About his wife and in my voice,

"She came to me and said
It would be all right, and we both knew
That wasn't going to be true for
A long time, if ever." She was that way.

People drift, it happens, I say.
"Not friends, not true friends,"
You're saying. And I have to agree.
You can call this nothing but a dream,
Which it was, or you can call it a vision,
But I know he was there and my voice
Was his and his voice was mine
And nothing was going to change
Here or in the afterlife, where we both
Will one day be, and maybe we'll shoot
Hoops again or lift a beer and toast
To time passing, past, and never to come
Again, such was that night, that fell on me
Like a hood over my falcon head
As I dreamed of flying up and away
Where Hank was there in the clearing
I was destined to rediscover on account of
Something I can never undo, which was
My life and his life, and friends that
Turned in other directions from each other
In a world that no longer exists.

"You must think there's some consolation,"
I say speaking for you. "You must think
You can fix things like they were.
You must think I'm interested in
Being in your dreams." Which okay, yes, I did.
Abandoning this world took you a lifetime,

Which you did as only you could do
And for me to remember at midnight
which is where you're something like alive.

# WHILE YOU'RE OUT OF TOWN (AGAIN)

You are gone a few days, again,
California, Bali, somewhere, Mars.
I'll cling to my hyperbaric chamber,
Don't you worry, I'll probably be okay.

I thought to take advantage of
The freedom and time to rewrite
The collected poems of Tennyson,
You know, the Charge of the Light
Brigade guy, no problem, Princess.

Once that was done, and after I
Discovered cool new elements to add
To the Periodic Table, I took up
Racing with that sweet Ferrari I stole.

It did get boring after a while,
Till the trek up Kilimanjaro,
And my critical update on the male gaze
(Pro and con and what the heck is that),
As imaged on my smart phone,
Which I have also redesigned.
This may take a few minutes,
Do not restart your device (or mine).

You out of town (again). You're right
We could use a break, I'm a handful,

But I still miss our midnight chats
Outside casement windows where late
The vampire vixens yearn to congregate.

Your name's all over this new opera of mine.
I'm the tenor in the wings waiting in sable for a sign,
Ready to hit the high notes for you, waiting for
The orchestra to strike up for you,
So you might drift becostumed onstage like you owned it,
Which you definitely, most definitely do,
Unless you steal the stage once more. In which case,
Please bring it back along with yourself,
As there's no reason to sing an aria except with you
Once you finally come home again (again).

# ODE TO THE LAST AUTHOR OF AN ODE (ME)

Minus an accountable moon and a spooky urn,
I espy the rollicky meadows intimate and sere,
The grove teeming with song-drunk birds,
All streams running dead to ground.
So much for the 24/7 internet news beat.
All I lament is the chilly lamentations of
The night, and here it is high noon
In California, where screenplays outnumber raindrops
And that's okay, even if no ode horizons for me now.
The Sirens tethered to my inbox tempt
Me to affirm my fate, which I never knew was mine.
Things which I have seen I now can see no more.
And if I come upon shepherds hard at work—
Admittedly a very long shot in my hood—
I'll be sure to ask how I can lend a hand,
I'll ask if I was ever here or how I ever knew
Shepherds in poetry did once abound,
As they'd pipe and play and drumbeat the creaturely sound.
What to make of an old-fashioned dread
Of old-fashionedness? The quiet of the house
Surrounds, familiarity of all that's strange
About time that unrelents and ecstasies on the edge,
Bliss that unforgets a passing word of
Someone passing by or passing through, but
Instead it's only you who knows who you are,
Who's no longer there, if you or I ever were.

Birds populate my room, shimmering crimson wings,
Reminiscent of a dream-drenched typhoon long ago,
Another war, another age, another me,
And their songs, first drafts of suicide notes,
So sweet, so mournful, suffused with a message
Not to follow their lead, whatever we do.
There's no consolation commensurate with desire.
Still, words form at the back of my throat,
Where thoughts lie just deep enough for tears.

# NEW PEN

To write in pencil is to revel in fear,
It's to turn from joy, from falling in love, from desire.
Better watch out now, hello, my new pen.
It contains all the plays, all the poems, in theory,
Though the pen itself is anti-theoretical as
That quinoa salad I just ordered at the shop.
Whatever possessed me to order the quinoa,
A word I just learned how to pronounce, though
This pen has no trouble, it delights in writing *quinoa,*
*Quinoa, quinoa* all up and down the page.
Quinoa, a pretty enough word, I admit—someday
It may be a food source I love a little as well.
But let's get back to my beautiful new pen.
Oh, and just now I changed out the black ink
For the Pacific blue refill. Man, this pen.
It contains all the pay-to-the-order-ofs
In the world, all the signed seven-figure deals
That will not come in electronically anymore,
Which I deplore, though not the mythical seven-
Figure deals themselves, which I am good with.
I'll confess, all right? I used to prefer my trusty
Mechanical pencil to any pen. But I have to accept
My fate. True, I stole this pen when the clerk
Turned away to call the cops on loitering-suspiciously-me,
Smart clerk, though not as quick as me.
Now nothing can stop me, not even handcuffs,
From leaving my ink on all the pages that lurk.

# HOW I EVER GOT OVER MYSELF

I don't know who's writing this anymore.
I could say that proved a relief, a blessing,
Till I realized I'm no longer involved.
I started waiting on tables in random eateries,
Content with 10 percent tips and snarky Yelp reviews.
Try it sometime, but only after doing cleanup
For parties you'd never be invited to in your life.
Take up a new mantra. Borrow one if you must.
Write a dozen snail mail missives to creditors.
Go to high school reunions whenever you can,
Especially high schools you did not attend.
Tell the class president you once had a crush
And they never looked more beautiful than tonight.
Rush off to the pound and rescue all the pits,
Take the broken-winged blackbird to the vet ER.
Gather up all fallen leaves wherever they fall,
But first lie down in their bed and just breathe.
Since I'm now completely over myself,
I've finally landed on my personal pronoun.
Which is, you guessed it, *you.*
Thank you for the essential nonexistent support,
I'll take the answer to my question off the air.

# CHRONIC CONDITION

Oh, I breathe into the pain, own my pain all right,
Meditate, I'm told. I can take a pill, of course
I could, but the pain would still be there, pain
Like a weather one town over, squalls
Heading over next break in the clouds.
Pain like a forest of pines, while walking beneath
The canopy, putting one foot in front of another,
The cones littering the floor, blue jays going nuts,
Hoot owl calls flute into my brain.
My pain makes for no colors, it screams black,
The absence of color, go ahead tell my pain that.
A darkness lit up from within itself.
You can't cut down all the trees. I mean
You could try, but you'd be left with vanishment
Of trees alongside the excrescences
Of impossible to forget pain, which is chronic,
Like life is chronic, until it isn't, a truth
Which leaves one lacking in satisfaction.
No use changing your food program, don't
Call it a diet, though I don't know why I can't,
And besides, there's nothing but pain. Pain like
A hunger, pain like the queasiness that rushes in
On waves inside, pain, the unreachable bread
On the far side of the pastoral table where
Loved ones collect, gathering inside the knots
Twisting of pain. You could flip over the table

Sometimes, you could, but what would that do?
Pain like a sandcastle on the heaving shore.
You could throw yourself into the churn of surf,
You could, and you might, but then—but then.
Scenes cycle in your brain, and for a while
It's all calm, in the city where you'd been a child
And gamboled on green fields before pain settled in
And introduced you to time, an old friend, an intimate
You need never to have known, but then again, you did,
Because look, pain walks with you into the white light,
Flickering, looping, gorgeous, your name inscribed.

# LEGEND OF PETE, PETE CROSS

If ever I had a friend in my life it would have been
Pete, Pete Cross. He kept a low profile, truth be told,
And once he was known as Chris, Chris Cross.
But anybody could tell what would go wrong with
A name like that. Alex, Alex Cross, he tried for a while,
But he didn't feel it, did old Pete, Pete Cross.
I could tell you things about him, if I knew anything,
But then he kept to himself, social media being
What it is, flowing with mis- and disinformation,
Spoofing and spamming and so on, terms
He did not understand at all, though he might have.
Once he got ten guys to pack into a phone booth
And made the local news beat, but he had no
Follow-up second act once phone booths disappeared.
He was a funny guy, Pete, Pete Cross, and for
The record he was never Peter, Peter Cross. No,
They baptized him Pete, and that was fine with him.
And with me, I hasten to add. I would have said
Chris, Chris Cross has possibility, and made my case.
You might consider him an Enlightenment Thinker.
Two pints in, he would quote Sir Isaac Newton,
About seeing farther by standing on shoulders of giants.
Newton discovered the laws of gravity, and Pete,
Pete Cross never let go. If you weighed one hundred
Pounds on Earth, you would weigh seventeen on the moon.
"Think about it, man," he'd say. "Just think about it."

That's my Pete, Pete Cross, though he was hardly mine.
We are all mysteries to each other, aren't we? And we
Are pulled to each other, howsoever the earth resists,
Our gravitational force field compelling us closer,
Even if we never once grasped each other at all.

# THIS IS MY DEPRESSED FACE

This? Oh, this is my Depressed Face,
Which, quite right, fine, needs work.
I have other faces if you care
And especially if you do not.
How about this one, my
Had A Good Day for a Change
Face? Okay, I'll fix it next time.
A big hit at the club was
I'm Seeing Somebody New
Face, which comes in several
Varieties. Sparkling baby blues,
Bleached teeth, trimmed beard,
Chin up. Now, seasons may factor in.
Rosey cheeks, winter time, Vail.
Not that I've ever set foot in Vail.
I just keep that winter face going
Year-long, because that's how it is,
See the top line above, if you will,
Or if you won't. Meanwhile this is
The face for taking in all the bad news
That time, all the time, hearing about
Who left who for you can't be serious,
About who drove off the road, the cliff,
About whose chemo did not work magic,
About who lost their shirt in the crash—
Which crash? Take your pick, pal.

Oh, the list goes on and on, so many,
It's useful to have backup inventory,
All the faces raring to go, any occasion,
Like one for the night stroll, looking up, street
Lamps, wondering why there's any reason
To have a face to meet anybody un-
Expected, when that's the one person
I'm pumped up to greet, Hey, it's me,
I think. It's me, right? Oh, and this is my
Deep Thinker face—still working on that one.
My go-to face you know all too well, here's
I'd Crawl on my Knees Across the Mojave
For You. Right, you're seeing that one
Right now, right here, don't turn away.

# HEY, FUNNY STORY

About the time Joe Di Prisco—not me, another Joe Di Prisco—
Made his appearance with the band he did not know
He was in. Those were the days, and the nights.
Jazz standards, pop covers, like that. Dinner jacket,
Bow tie, shiny shoes, pomade slathered into his hair,
Even though lots of guys weren't doing that anymore
And he wasn't Black, either, as far as he knew.
He lit up a cigarette and leaned against
The baby grand and blew smoke rings up
Into the chandelier. True story: he never did
Smoke a single cigarette in his life, I mean the Joe
I was and maybe still am, though as for the other
Joe, jury's out, and I'm keeping myself out of this dream
Till further notice. Fly me to the moon, he sang,
And up the lazy river, and what kind of fool am I,
Rakishly untying his bow tie and singing his heart out,
Moon river, wider than a mile, crossing you in style,
With what was left of his heart, and there she was
Solo at her cocktail table, sipping a Brandy Alexander,
Her signature drink, as he might have recalled.
She is plainly in love with the other Joe Di Prisco
And not with this one, who is me, even though I am
Singing only to and for her, witchcraft, crazy
Witchcraft, strictly taboo. What kind of drink is
Brandy Alexander, which looks medicinal, and the night
Promises to never end, and this band of mine is drifting

Into I'll be seeing you, misty, autumn leaves,
I sing to myself what a wonderful world.
This song is dedicated, says the other Joe, to
The lovely lady right there in the rustling blue silk
Dress, here you go, darling, what's your name,
And she goes *Joe Di Prisco*. I tell you, man,
Some nights it's dangerous to dream, and she goes,
All nights are dangerous to dream. What a world
Wonderful, overrun with a legion of Joes, and I'm
Just here, not singing at all, working the lights, as
Last call at the bar goes out, and all the Joes in town
Turn out to be me after all, who knew, besides Joe
And the girl sipping on her drink waiting for her cue?

# BUCKET LIST

Face-up underneath a waterfall, handmade shoes.
Catching the Coho salmon, letting them go.

Marauding through all-night markets,
Making at dawn your wished-for meal.

Returned at last to that childhood park,
Swinging up unto sunset and beyond.

Phone ringing, me picking up, you at last.
The sheen on a hummingbird's wings.

Ball in midair, the dogs leaping up,
Framed by slanted sun between olive trees.

High mountain trestle, train stuck in snow.
The secret of life, the worst-kept secret,
Which is, there's no kind of secret at all.

Gone back to a meadow stretched out in dreams,
Millions of poppies up into the tree line.

Wandering with horses, cows in bright oblivion,
Hearing what the horses are telling me,
Knowing what they mean is all true.

And here forever comes, with me in my own arms,
Where I've never felt at home until now.

Hopelessly hopeful, resigned to resignation,
Cold under the cascade, deluged by what's to come.

The myth I was once alive may be summoned up,
While I am cupping waterfall, waterfall, the waterfall.

# SO NOW THAT YOU'VE BEEN DIAGNOSED!

We are currently serving other patients, thank you for calling.
If this is a medical or psychological emergency, hang up
And dial 911. We will take your call in the order in which
It was received, please hold, do not hang up, your wait
Is approximately who knows? We have no idea. Of course,
This is a lot for you to take in. You have your frequently
Unasked questions that tambourine against your brainpan.
Search our site for latest medical breakthroughs.
Doubts wrangle around like crawfish in the pot on the stove.
We'll always be here for you, 24/7, at least for stretches of
Weekday mornings. Ignore the chatter and comparable experience
Tales told by terminally well-meaning mopes who swing
On the family tree or inside the office breakroom. We know
What *we* might do, not that we're here with advice, and your calls
May be recorded for retraining purposes. Let's first agree,
Keep the Dalai Lama the fuck out of this. What was that?
If we were you—wait a second, do we look like your *mother*?
Which means we're not you—but if we were: Some say
Rippling koi ponds are good for gloaming-hour reflection,
Some, the owls that hoot each to each across the dark,
Some, reading clouds that drift above the bleached hills
Across an otherwise apricot expanse of sky, and they're all
Solid options as far as they go. We understand why you seek,
No disrespect, a second opinion. For our money (and we are
Seriously underpaid, don't forget), stick with shoreline birds,
Who are sublimely indifferent to the diagnosis that is you.

Sitting on the shore is good for incorporating this news
If you ask us, which we told you don't do, pay attention,
But now we're back on the line till we lose the connection,
Thanks for holding, we're underwater, legions out there diagnosed,
Where were we? Right: the seashore we were just talking about
When you were not listening. On the shore, keep locked in
On the seagulls, the terns, the pelicans, and especially the snowy
Egrets and great blue herons, which are easily confused,
As you are these days, naturally, because this is a lot for you to take in.
See how they fish in the tidal mudflats? Count on us, we are a team,
Your personal posse of care providers. And then there are the gulls
And pelicans that dive-bomb into the surf, sometimes coming up
Empty, sometimes fat. That's one lesson perfectly wasted on
The likes of us. Like us, you have much to learn about surveillance
And impermanence. If you'd prefer to leave us a voice mail,
We pledge to someday call you back, because, sure,
The canned music gets old fast, another reason to walk the shore.
It will cross your mind—Dalai Lama or no: Change your diet,
Give the vodka a rest, take up Tai Qi. All excellent resolves,
But still your thoughts reel and toss like tumbleweed
In sandstorms across the Mojave floor. You're really taking in
A lot, we know. Yes, we did say that before, and we'll say it again,
And hours from now it'll still be true. The new pathology report
Is available for viewing in your personal folder, access through
Your Personal Record Number (PRN). Please update your password,
Which we've rejected (*URdead2me*, come on). We permit
No member of our award-winning staff to use the term
*Irony* in your immediate vicinity, keep us posted.
The physical body is not physical, and beyond the reach of regret,
Remorse. So hold close to the shoreline, where nobody will remark
They know better than you what you are going through.
Birds will never say that. They're too busy in midair or aswim,
Without a single follow-up appointment beyond the sea, beyond flight,

Beyond being caught up in the swells of dissolving time. The sea goes
On and on and on, as we—and especially now you—will not,
And the seabirds' second opinion is to let go of what's to come
That was never meant to be. Your wait time is more than any of us
Can bear. Leave a message and we will call you back,
When you're finally ready to listen.

# WINDY NIGHT WALK TO THE SEA

The trees have raptured the herons, who can fault them,
Which is where you would light if you sprout wings.

Darkness swells, and your three brothers, long gone,
Emerge. It's good to see them, even if you can't,

To hear their voices rise in rhythm with
The slip and crash of the surf, even if you don't.

They have secrets to divulge you never will learn,
Which always was the case. Turns out you can love

Without understanding or being understood.
To remember is the charge of those left behind.

To be remembered, a charm the dead bequeath.
*Where you've been is where I'll go*, you say,

Step by step, down to the sea. You see the ruins
Beneath the sea, where you cannot help but see yourself.

On this night, you're four boys in the world again,
But it's all on you, on your own lifelong pilgrimage,

To survive if you can, though no one does, the sea,
All ways tonight leading down to the shore.

332

And wait, just look, you want to tell them, the air
Shudders as if with the millioned migration of

Black butterflies, and you follow them following you
Everywhere, and everywhere, everywhere's the sea.

# LAST LEG ON THE STARLIKE

Feels like forever on the Starlike Express.
Revelations rush past, *click-clack, click-clack*:
Factory abandoned, school boarded-up,
Peeling eucalyptus, riverbank scorched.

Faded billboards' come-and-get-it: E-Z Loans,
Pomo Casino, escorts, loose slots, *click-clack*,
Jesus Saves. White-haired woman in a nightgown,
Dancing in the poppy field, waving to no one.

You lift an arm—you know how it is—and wave back.
That's when the observation coach fills with
Strangers who know much more than you do
About yourself—family's inevitable even here.

You poach the haunted stare of the hunted,
Chewing their trapped legs free. No wonder
The buzzed conductor—pencil moustache,
Pillbox hat, pocket watch, smirk—bears a grudge.

So you exchange furtive looks with the femme
Fatale and study the natty assassin who picks
His teeth, terminal suave. Seems like diamond heist
Could be in the offing, insurgents lie in wait, *click-clack*.

Give us the combination, the runaway pleads.
You would if you knew. Her black eyes make you wish
She'd commandeer the engine, seize the trestle,
Sing an anthem, unfurl a patchwork flag. She disappears.

Screeching into station, your heart syncs and arrests.
Feels like this could pass for your destination,
Something tells you, and you ought to declaim in
Icelandic, French, or German, though no, no, you can't.

Conductor, killer, femme, world without end, you.
Feels like you're understanding why at last.
You journey to forget what you had to flee,
You escape to remember where you have to be.

As the Starlike lurches forward, leaves the station,
Another train's arriving on the opposite track.
In the glow of that cabin you catch sight of what
You suspected: it's you, *there*, destined elsewhere again.

Locomoting through endless sunset serrated, aflame,
You yearn for sleep, for darkness to hurry up bloom
Behind your eyes. A man in transit *click-clack*, you greet
All those perched under stars in the fleeting trees.

But then, a theme park appears. What you would give
To have a theme of your own. But count on pyrotechnics,
Water cannon volleys, vertigo carousel, bumper cars,
A whistling calliope. And at the Ferris wheel top
It has to be you, holding your breath before the drop.

## POSTSCRIPT:
## IT'S ALWAYS BEEN POETRY
## (BECAUSE EVEN WHEN IT WASN'T, IT WAS)

What I have learned and what I know for sure is that life is very long except when it's very short, and it just might be both, and at the same time.

With that in mind, I recall that I wrote poems when I was younger, and after not writing poems for a long time, I wrote poems when I was not. What I mean is, there was a break of about two decades that passed unnoticed by everyone, except, that is, by me. That's why the subtitle of this book fills out like this: *New & Collected Poems: 1971–1980 / 1999–2023.*

That / is doing a lot of work here.

I do not attribute this break to writer's block, mainly because I do not believe in such a condition. It wasn't a period of self-imposed monastic silence, either, but if it were, that would have been a clamorous mosh pit of an abbey. (Right after high school, as a matter of fact, I did enter a Catholic novitiate and briefly became Brother Joseph, another story unto itself.) There were better professional moves to make along the way, I'm positive, though career considerations have religiously eluded me. I also do not think of this as interruption or hiatus, because that could imply mishap or strategic planning. For the record that nobody's keeping, I did not devote myself to windsurfing or bond trading or white-collar crime, and I didn't join a cult or tend a vineyard, but it's complicated—because I did once make a living playing cards around the world for a few years and even running restaurants. Along the way, I did complete graduate school and taught for many years and cowrote books about child development. I also founded a not-for-profit, New Literary Project, which is thriving, but that was born in 2015.

Truth is, there did take up residence in town my own personal carnivale, whose main attractions revolved around disasters and demons and disturbances of one stripe and another. Not to overdramatize or minimize anything, but those are the sorts of disruptions one might endure who lives long enough, all the while slowly learning or, in my case, re-learning how to live and how to write, which may be variations on the same theme. I'll also spare the details pertaining to some unexpected, fortunate chances, unmerited gifts, and incredible surprises. More than anything, I feel absurdly lucky to have survived my extensive c.v. of questionable choices, and fortunate that there were people who cared more than I had a right to expect. In this context, I cannot resist noting in passing I'm ambivalently pleased and curious about the poet, then in his early twenties, whose work appears in this collection under my name. I have to wonder if he would recognize the one he may have never been destined to become.

In the grand scheme of things, after all, there may be no grand scheme of things, and writing a poem may amount to an act of disruption in and of itself.

Nonetheless, the arc of the trajectory that is mine may be traceable in two memoirs I wrote, *Subway to California* (2014) and *The Pope of Brooklyn* (2017), or even in my novels published since 2000. Perhaps, however, it's all too simple. The explanation for the arrival of any poem or poet is or is not to be found, for better or worse, in the poem itself. Beyond that, maybe nothing can account for the rupture that creates the opening for a poem—or for that matter, the lifetime of a poet represented in his Collected Poems.

In certain moods it feels like there was this moment I never saw coming, between when I stopped writing poems and before I began again, when I was waiting and waiting and waiting for the next line to materialize. Only somehow then it did, and I wrote it down, just in the nick of time.

*Summer 2023*

**GRATEFUL THANKS** to the editors of magazines where many of these poems originally appeared, sometimes in different form and under different titles:

*88*: "End of an Age."

*The American Reader*: "My Last Résumé," "The Ringling Bros Barnum and My Family Circus."

*Berkeley Poetry Review*: "Double Feature," "The Idea of a Garden," "Negligible."

*Blue Unicorn*: "Poem in which Orpheus rearranges the world yet again."

*The Cincinnati Review*: "The Satrap Will See You Now."

*Epoch*: "My Father Declares Bankruptcy."

*failbetter*: "So Now That You've Been Diagnosed!"

*Fine Madness*: "Poem in which he often is drowning," "Poem in which he has trouble with this elegy for Bathsheba's first husband, Uriah, a loyal soldier whose death in war was neatly arranged by King David, who would become her second," "Poem in which appear the special children," "Poem in which there is the ultomato, as well as his grandfather, and where he comes close to quoting Gertrude Stein, *Picasso*: 'When he ate a tomato the tomato was not everybody's tomato.'"

*Fog and Light*: "The Bar at the End of Some Other Road."

*Forklift, Ohio*: "Sleep Is/Is Not a Lost Cause," "Plums of My Imaginary Daughter" [#18 "Brief Biography of an Imaginary Daughter"].

*Italian Americana*: "Ultomato."

*Kayak*: "The Beautiful Wounds, "Objet d'Art," "Philosophy 1-A: The Wisdom of the West," "Poem in which no one appears to show up for his party."

***March Hares: Best Poems of Fine Madness***: "Poem in which he has trouble with this elegy for Bathsheba's first husband, Uriah, a loyal soldier whose death in war was neatly arranged by King David, who would become her second," "Poem in which appear the special children."

***Midwest Quarterly***: "Poem in which he devours a white wolf," "Poem in which illustrious Occam shaves."

***Pebble***: "Man with Gestures," "Mea Culpa for My Life in Syracuse."

***Poetry Daily***: "Adventures in Language School"

***Poetry Foundation***: #1-5 from "Brief Biography of an Imaginary Daughter," "Emperor with No Clothes," "Reasons Nobody Ever Called a Good Book of Poems a Page-Turner," "My Last Résumé."

***Poetry Northwest***: "For My Contracepted Children," "The Dumb Page," "Meditation on the Angels," "Poem in which he faces a firing squad after weeks of reading Latin American fiction," "Poem in which he directs a pretentious, critically acclaimed low-budget movie even though it's obvious he's never even been to film school," "The Son's Poem," "Starlike," "Teaching the Children," "When It Takes Place."

***Poetry Now***: "Poem in which he looks past the problems of relationship and forges ahead dreamily."

***Prairie Schooner***: "Drunken Conversation," "Poem in which we hear news from the Far West."

***Remington Review***: "28 June 1973," "The Sad Tropic," "Open Heart Surgery," "Poem in which an escape takes place."

***Rivers of Earth and Sky***: "My Mission Statement."

***Sycamore Review***: "Poem in which he demonstrates your influence upon his life," "Poem in which he recalls those precious journeys with Wanda."

*Syracuse Poems:* "The Dumb Page."

*Third Coast:* "Poem in which the concept of closure is addressed."

*Threepenny Review:* "Poem in which he depends upon a passing familiarity with baseball and the works of Sir Walter Scott."

*Zyzzyva:* "Adventures in Language School," "I Was Just Leaving," "More Elements of Style," "My Mission Statement," "Reasons Nobody Ever Called a Good Book of Poems a Page-Turner," "Symptomatology," "There Comes a Time There Comes a Time, Or: Go Forth."

# ACKNOWLEDGMENTS

### *Thank you,*

Diane Del Signore
Tyson Cornell
John A. Gray
Mario Di Prisco
Kim Dower
Laura Cogan
Beth Spencer
Don Bogen
Diane Frank
David Breskin
Rupert & the Hounds: Abby & Jack & Edwina; Ava & Raylan


*In memoriam*
George P. Elliott, Josephine Miles, David Wagoner, Dean Young